The (Guilty) Conscience of a Conservative

The (Guilty) Conscience of a Conservative

Craig Schiller

ARLINGTON HOUSE·PUBLISHERS
NEW ROCHELLE, NEW YORK

Schiller, Craig, 1951-
    The (guilty) conscience of a conservative.

    Includes bibliographical references and index.
    1.   Conservatism—United States.   I.   Title
JA84.U5S35   320.5'2'0973   78-1297
ISBN 0-87000-383-6

P10   9   8   7   6   5   4   3   2   1

Manufactured in the United States of America

To
L. BRENT BOZELL
and the editors of *Triumph,*
who taught the American Right
that there is more to conservatism
than the Tenth Amendment

Contents

Acknowledgements

I wish to take this opportunity to thank my editor, Mr. Richard E. Band of Arlington House, for his encouragement and assistance throughout the writing of this volume. In addition, the prompt and courteous help of the staff of the Finkelstein Memorial Library in Spring Valley, New York, and of its Inter-Library Loan Department in particular, was greatly appreciated.

An Apology

"In unity there is strength." This wise maxim has too often gone unheeded by conservatives. The history of the Right is clouded over with frequent displays of self-defeating internecine warfare. One need only recall, in this vein, the consistent inability of European counterrevolutionaries of both the corporate nationalist and monarchial restorationist schools of thought to come to terms with each other and offer a unified rightist alternative in their respective countries. American conservatives have similarly engaged in numerous and at times exceptionally vicious internal struggles, as individualists have feuded with Burkeans, "conservative moderates" with the "far right," and so on. Instead of getting down to their prime obligation in this crucial epoch of world history—which is, obviously, to defeat the forces of leftism—rightists seem content

9

to squander their intellectual and practical efforts on holier-than-thou criticism of their comrades-in-arms.

Many conservative setbacks are directly traceable to this distinct tendency of rightists to promote their own private denominations of conservatism at the expense of the common good. Whether we are talking about the failure of the different elements of the French Right to pull together during the turbulent events in Paris on February 6, 1934, or the startling reluctance of leading American conservatives to support the presidential-primary campaign of Governor Ronald Reagan, the rightist performance in the public forum has been severely hampered by this conservative weakness of losing sight of one's primary objectives.

It is therefore with a certain degree of trepidation that I offer the following volume to the public. In the pages to come many leading conservative politicians and thinkers, periodicals and organizations, will be scrutinized and criticized. I sincerely hope, though, that these criticisms will not be misinterpreted. My intention is not to add yet another title to the list of "my conservatism *über alles*" books. Heaven knows, we have seen enough of these in recent decades. On the contrary, one of the major themes of this work is that there exists a core level of unity among all the varying forms of legitimate rightism, despite their apparent differences. In order to explain the nature of this unity and to offer what I hope is helpful advice on the basis of it, I have sometimes found it necessary to chide certain rightists who, by virtue of their sincere and often even profound devotion to only *one* aspect of conservatism, have hurt the movement. The reader is urged to keep in mind that the conservative shortcomings discussed here stem merely from doctrinal incompleteness or from an unrealistic approach to practical politics. These are not serious errors in a moral sense, but as will be amply shown later, they have proved extremely damaging on the practical level. King Solomon speaks in the *Proverbs* of an "open reproof" that issues forth from "hidden love." It is in this spirit that the reader should interpret the volume he now holds.

1 The Great Retreat

Shortly after Richard Nixon's overwhelming victory over George McGovern in the 1972 presidential election, several mainstream[1] thinkers of the American Right cast a long, hard glance in the mirror and attempted to size up the successes and failures of the postwar conservative movement. Commenting on the Republican landslide and the prospects of four more years of Nixonism, *National Review* called attention to the fact that

> American conservatism has been largely smothered as a distinctive doctrine and movement . . . Those who still think of themselves as conservative face the duty of reviewing and re-evaluating what they believe and what they do, and this is a job that belongs on the immediate agenda.[2]

As R. Emmett Tyrrell, editor of the *Alternative* (lately renamed the *American Spectator*) and favorite of young American rightists, expressed it in a letter to *National Review* on December 8, 1972, American conservatism suffers from "a continual political drift."[3] That the once clearly spelled-out doctrines of American conservatism have become extremely blurred was acknowledged by William F. Buckley, Jr., the generally recognized symbolic leader of the

11

intellectual Right in America, as early as 1969 when he wrote of a "new conservatism"[4] that had emerged to take the place of the "old conservatism" of the fifties, adopting "new forms"[5] and "different . . . positions"[6] from those of its predecessor.

Unfortunately, conservative thinkers did not pause long enough to examine exactly how much the movement had, in fact, evolved since the days of its rebirth in the late forties and subsequent further articulation in the fifties and early sixties. It would probably be a highly sobering experience for contemporary rightists to take down from their shelves that classic work of early conservatism, *The Conscience of a Conservative* by Senator Barry Goldwater, or even the somewhat more serene (and probably therefore considerably less popular) work of Senator John Tower of Texas, *A Program for Conservatives,* and examine the positions advanced therein. (Perhaps the Arizonan and Texan themselves could similarly benefit by rereading their earlier works.) For the "bourgeois conservatism" of the seventies (the phrase is Donald Atwell Zoll's)[7] has largely repudiated the major principles of the early rightist revival. I use the word principles, as opposed to policies or programs, because the abandonment of fifties conservatism by the leading rightist thinkers of the seventies appears to have basic philosophical significance. It is not merely that conservatives no longer call for unleashing the 500,000 Nationalist Chinese troops to attack the mainland; no longer call for invading Cuba, tearing down the Berlin wall, or liberating Albania (to cite a few random examples from the litany of conservative foreign-policy proposals twenty years ago). Rather, they seem no longer cognizant of the underlying philosophical commitment that originally led them to embrace these positions. This commitment was based upon the belief that, to quote Frank Meyer in 1958:

> We have to recognize what the Communists know and openly proclaim, that Communism and Western civilization cannot both survive.[8]

On a deeper level fifties conservatives believed with Frederick Wilhelmsen that

> the West today has lost the courage to face up to the only political end which can really interest any decent man in the second half of the twentieth century: the business of beating Communism or getting beaten at the try.[9]

12

Sentiments such as these are not the stuff of which pragmatic compromise politics is made. Accordingly, conservative politicians felt with Senator Tower that the goal of American international strategy should be "the vanquishment of Communism,"[10] or as *National Review* summed things up in its "Credenda," which appeared in the journal's maiden issue:

> The century's most blatant force of satanic utopianism is communism. We consider "coexistence" with communism neither desirable nor possible, nor honorable; we find ourselves irrevocably at war with communism and shall oppose any substitute for victory.[11]

It is only reasonable to suspect upon reading statements such as the foregoing that when the leading intellectuals of the Right surrendered the practical proposals of fifties conservatism, they began hedging on the root assumptions of the movement as well. William F. Buckley, Jr. admitted as much when he wrote in 1969 that "somewhere along the line" since Khrushchev's visit to America in 1959,

> the word had gone out, and its force on conservatives was not lost, that it is vulgar to raise one's voice against the Communists.

Therefore, concluded the editor of *National Review*, "conservatives . . . look for new forms with which to express themselves." What precisely should these "new forms" of conservatism be? Buckley gave three examples: (1) defense of the democratic process, (2) defense of due process of law, and (3) defense of "upward [economic] mobility."[12] In 1975 the man who probably contributed more than any other rightist to the resurgence of the movement was still explaining this "new conservatism" and contrasting it to that of *National Review*'s earlier years. Interviewed by Lee Edwards of *Conservative Digest*, Buckley declared:

> More and more I find that the challenge that we face at *National Review*, and all conservatives face, is to lay down the distinction between their way of life and our own way of life.
>
> It's one thing to say, okay, the Ukraine is going to stay under Communist despotism for as long as I can see into the future. It's not going to be liberated in any way which we thought it might be 25 years ago. But it is another thing to say

as some people are saying, for instance, about China, that life
there is preferable to life here.[13]

It would seem at first glance (we shall shortly return to the
matter in greater detail) that conservatism in the seventies finds
itself stripped of both its former programs and its theoretical first
principles. Rightists cannot have it both ways. Either the "only
decent thing to do" is to vanquish satanic utopianism or, alternatively, one opts for coexistence, which was once considered
"neither desirable, nor possible." There is no philosophical common ground upon which the crusading anti-Communism of the
fifties can stand with Buckley's call for an elucidation of the benefits of Anglo-Saxon liberties, however worthwhile such an endeavor most assuredly is.

The retreat is clearly documented (although it is not the author's
intention to do so) in George Nash's recent book *The Conservative
Intellectual Movement in America since 1945.*[14] This book traces
the theoretical development of the American right wing from the
late forties, when conservatism was an almost totally forgotten
persuasion in America, up to the present day. In the process it
demonstrates with vivid clarity how the conservative position on
issues like foreign policy, internal security, free enterprise, and
constitutional interpretation has radically changed over the past
three decades. Nash, however, is determined to draw optimistic
conclusions about the future of American conservatism from the
data he has assembled; so, except for a few soul-searching passages,[15] his study pays little attention to the phenomenon of "respectable"[16] conservatism's continually receding profile, which
emerges unmistakably from his history of the movement.

Let us now document in some detail the history of the conservatives' retreat from their firm stands of the fifties, which places them
today in virtual agreement with the positions of fifties liberalism.
Most of what is to follow has already been said by L. Brent Bozell,
the editor of *Triumph* magazine (which recently ceased publication). Bozell charged that American conservatives had, during the
1964–68 period, "simply abandoned" the basic propositions of the
movement. He spelled out this analysis in the March 1969 issue of
Triumph in an open letter to American rightists entitled "Letter to
Yourselves." Without attempting to define conservatism, choosing
instead to describe it empirically as it "has 'come on' to the country
as a political movement . . . after World War II," he outlined the
basic positions of the movement as follows:

14

There is *anti-statism*, as represented by Taft. There is *nationalism*, as represented by MacArthur. There is *anti-communism*, as represented by (Joseph) McCarthy. The fourth is *constitutionalism*, which has never had a champion of the status of the others, but which may be recalled by thinking of Bricker, or more recently Thurmond.[17]

Bozell went on to observe that "on every front" where conservatives have confronted the Left they have seen their basic assumptions defeated:

Consider . . . your campaign against big government, against Keynesian economics, against compulsory welfare; your defense of states' rights and the constitutional prerogatives of Congress; your struggle for a vigorous anti-Soviet foreign policy; your once passionate stand for the country's flag and its honor. Is there a single field where the secular liberals have had to yield . . . ?[18]

William F. Buckley, Jr., commenting (quite critically) on the "Letter to Yourselves," said in 1971:

To which dirge Mr. Bozell might have added, had he been writing two years later. Consider your stand against Communist China; your opposition to unbalanced budgets; your resentment of Supreme Court decisions that transfer the First Amendment into an anti-religious instrument of Bolshevik ruthlessness.[19]

Bozell, with Buckley's help, has outlined the dimensions of the conservative retreat in broad detail. In order to demonstrate the essential truth of his thesis, it will be necessary to trace the conservative stand on some sample issues from the fifties to the present. I have selected the areas of civil rights and foreign policy, key issues during the past two decades to Americans in general and rightists in particular.

In its attitude to the Negro equal-rights movement, *National Review* magazine passed through three distinct stages of editorial policy. In its early years the magazine defended the Southern system, with its various forms of racial discrimination, on three grounds. First, because of "the median cultural superiority of white over Negro." In an August 24, 1957 editorial entitled "Why the South Must Prevail," *National Review* declared:

. . . a valid distinction exists between a culture pre-eminently white and one which would issue upon the political predominance of Southern Negroes in their present stage of development . . .[20]

On September 7 of that year "A Clarification" appeared:

National Review believes that the South's premises are correct. If the majority wills what is socially atavistic, then to thwart the majority may be, though undemocratic, enlightened . . .[21]

Second, the fifties conservatives were convinced that even if integration was sociologically or ethically desirable (this was Goldwater's position, and it seems to have been adopted by National Review in later years), still the federal government had no constitutional right to force the South to grant equal rights to Negroes, with the possible exception of the right to vote. Goldwater spelled out this position in his best-selling book The Conscience of a Conservative, when he wrote in relation to the famous Brown decision of the Supreme Court (which declared de jure segregated schools to be in violation of the Fourteenth Amendment):

It may be wise or just or expedient for Negro children to attend the same schools as white children, but they do not have a civil right to do so which is protected by the federal government.[22]

What were the Southern states to do in order to protect their sovereign rights? The 1964 GOP nominee, again in The Conscience, trumpeted the answer: massive noncompliance with the Court's decision, apparently through some form of the old doctrine of state "interposition" or "nullification" of federal laws. He wrote:

I therefore support all efforts of the states, excluding violence of course, to preserve their rightful powers over education.[23]

In 1957, when the South, in the person of Arkansas governor Orval Faubus, attempted to defy the Eisenhower administration's enforcement of the 1954 desegregation rulings, National Review,

16

while noting that the "situation in Little Rock [admits of] no just solution," emphatically supported the governor's action:

> Unless we are prepared to abandon the whole scheme of limited, mixed and divided sovereignty, we must defend Governor Faubus and his right and duty to preserve and defend the domestic peace of his state according to his oath of office.[24]

The third part of the rightist critique of the civil rights movement stressed that integration in the South ran contrary to the established customs, traditions, and mores of the region. It was therefore doomed to failure. On this basis conservatives concluded that even if integration was desirable on moral grounds, presumably even if enforcing it was a rightful prerogative of the federal government, it should still be rejected on pragmatic grounds as a utopian goal that the empirical evidence of the human condition showed to be unattainable. On September 9, 1956 *National Review* editorialized:

> In principle Liberalism rejects custom, revelation and tradition, in order to base its doctrine and program exclusively on reason . . .
> Now, school segregation is nonrational. Though it is possible to state arguments for segregation that are not anti-rational, the motives upon which it primarily rests are ancestral custom, deep feeling and time-honored prejudice. Yet many men and whole communities share the custom, feeling and prejudice, and may even believe that these are guides to the conduct of life more reliable than reason itself.
> . . . The cult of reason divorced from tradition and faith ends in the brute appeal to force . . .[25]

The fifties rightist supported the South in its efforts to defend the discriminatory system—on various grounds and in a lively and uncompromising style. By the early sixties, though, the syndrome of conservative retreat had already set in. In 1963, when George Wallace, then governor of Alabama, sought to thwart the federally ordered integration of the University of Alabama, using the same rhetoric and ideological justifications as did Governor Faubus in 1957, *National Review* was no longer enthusiastic. "The South," *NR* observed, "has clearly had it." As for Governor Wallace, there was no talk of his upholding his oath of office or "defending the whole scheme . . . of sovereignty" à la Faubus. On the contrary, *National Review* editorialized that the governor

> got off a pretty flat performance, and one which, moreover, evoked those awful spectacles of white children jeering at Negro children, riding the waves of undirected spite . . .[26]

Gone was the talk of customs and "time-honored prejudices." Gone were the fiery talk of the Tenth Amendment and the call for "interposition." In 1964 Goldwater also capitulated—publicly. Writing in his book *Where I Stand,* he amazingly maintained:

> In the schools the Attorney-General probably has the necessary authority through court decrees to effect integration . . . if more authority must be granted in this area, any additional legislation should be tightly drawn . . .[27]

By mid-1964, with their opposition to Negro suffrage and school desegregation long behind them, mainstream American conservatives retreated to their next line of defense: disapproval of the public accommodations and equal employment sections of the 1964 civil rights bill. By this time, though, traditional and empirical arguments against integration had ceased to be a part of the rightist apologetic. Everybody who was anybody on the American Right had long since gone on record as favoring equal rights in principle. (The only holdouts were a few Dixiecrats.) The last vestige of their once formidable structure of doctrine on civil rights that conservatives still spoke about was constitutionality. Indeed, on June 18, 1964, the day before he voted against the civil rights bill, Goldwater explained his position in an address to the Senate:

> I find no constitutional basis for the exercise of federal regulatory authority in either of these areas [public accommodations and employment]; and I believe the attempted usurpation of such power to be a grave threat to the very essence of our basic system of government . . .[28]

When Goldwater received the nomination, his platform pledged him to enforcement of the Civil Rights Act of 1964. In his public pronouncements during the campaign the senator supported this plank of his platform. Apparently Goldwater had abandoned his old position of advocating that states disobey "unconstitutional"

18

measures. Of course, political expediency may have dictated Goldwater's change of heart. But that was certainly no reason for *National Review* to relinquish its support for the Southern policy of massive noncompliance. James Jackson Kilpatrick (who during the heyday of the fifties called for using "every device of interposition" in opposition to "federal usurpations") wrote in a special section of *National Review* that appeared at the time of the 1964 Republican convention of San Francisco: "As President, Mr. Goldwater will be expected to enforce the 1964 law. The South must understand this."

All this was quite a comedown from the views Goldwater had put forth in *The Conscience,* where he called for, first, state defiance of the 1954 Supreme Court decision (which was "not the law of the land") and, second,

> a Constitutional amendment that would reaffirm the States' exclusive jurisdiction in the field of education.[29]

By 1964 Goldwater had reversed his logic. "If it is the wish of the American people" to extend the federal government's jurisdiction to include public accommodations and employment, he said, then "a constitutional amendment" was the way to do it.[30]

In any event, by the late sixties all the rightist fury that had been raised against *Brown,* against the Voting Rights Act, and against the civil rights bills of the mid-sixties was completely forgotten. *No* conservative spoke of "Negro inferiority," *no* conservative opposed universal suffrage for colored people, *no* conservative called for state nullification of *Brown,* much less of the Civil Rights Act of 1964. "Sociology," the Tenth Amendment, and "customs and feelings" were forgotten.

In May 1970, during an interview with *Playboy,* William F. Buckley, Jr. tried to revive the language of fifties conservatism's opposition to *Brown.* In examining his statement, though, it becomes apparent that the popular conservative polemicist was merely using the rhetoric of the "old conservatism" to defend a "new conservative" position, namely, the seventies rightist opposition to forced school integration through busing, quotas, and the like. He said:

> I continue to think it [*Brown*] was lousy law historically and analytically . . . There are unfortunately increased grounds for

believing that it was also bad sociology. Coerced massive integration is simply not working . . . checkerboarding the classroom [does not produce better education] . . .[31]

Of course, the *Brown* decision did not advocate "coerced massive integration" or "checkerboarding the classroom." It merely declared *de jure segregation* in the schools to be unconstitutional. Later court decisions broadened this doctrine to include forced busing as a remedy. The words of fifties conservatism were not really germane to the issue Buckley was discussing.

In recent years American conservatives have retreated further and further on the Negro question, defending other vantage points deeper in their own territory. They have attacked the violence and extremism of radical elements in the black community. They have denounced such leftist concepts as the collective guilt of Western civilization for its "persecution" of the Third World. They have opposed busing, quotas ("reverse discrimination"), and other manifestations of the egalitarianism of the seventies. Despite all their efforts in these directions, though, it was obvious that conservatives had moved away from the principles concerning civil rights that they had espoused in the fifties. With the exception of the "remnant" segment of the movement (see page 30), the position of seventies conservatives on questions of equal rights for blacks was, in the final analysis, indistinguishable from the antisegregation (*de jure*) stance of the liberalism of the fifties. In the seventies the editorial pages of *National Review* frequently made reference to articles written by fifties liberals in periodicals like *Commentary* and the *Public Interest,* for they, too, while opposing legally sanctioned discrimination, condemned the other extreme of quotas, affirmative action, busing, and so on. In the broad overview, one could say that as mainstream liberalism registered victory after victory over the Right in the fifties and sixties—on every issue from school desegregation to literacy tests—the Left moved on to advocate the various programs described today as "reverse discrimination." During this same period a small cadre of fifties liberals remained seemingly satisfied with the establishment of "equality of opportunity" as opposed to "equality of result." This group, typified by the *Commentary* and *Public Interest* writers, remained loyal to the programs of Adlai Stevenson and John Kennedy. Accordingly, when *National Review* and mainstream conservatives began their long retreat leftward, they met, ideologically, along the way this small group of (mostly Jewish) liberals still manning the guns of the old liberalism. The rightists liked the company of this group, so, to continue the metaphor, they set up camp with them, apparently unaware that they had once viewed their new habitat as a very bad place to be.

The area of foreign policy is another example of how the conservative game plan of the fifties has been shelved. I have already quoted the *National Review* "Credenda" on foreign policy, which centered on the principle of defeating Communism. Goldwater in *The Conscience* laid it out a bit more explicitly:

> The key guidepost [of U.S. foreign policy should be] the Objective, and we must never lose sight of it. It is not to wage a struggle against Communism, but to win it . . .[32]
>
> * * *
>
> . . . we [must] summon the will and the means for taking the initiative, and wage a war of attrition against [the Communists]—and hope thereby, to bring about the internal disintegration of the Communist empire.[33]

Although such a course, Goldwater conceded, "runs the risk of war," it was to be favored because it "holds forth the promise of victory." How was this goal of victory over Communism to be achieved? In a chapter of his book entitled "The Soviet Menace" he offered several specific proposals. He called for making NATO and SEATO into offensive alliances as opposed to their current posture, which he described as "completely defensive in nature and outlook."[34] "Foreign aid," he wrote, should be limited to "military and technical assistance to those nations . . . that are committed to a common goal of defeating world Communism."[35] He called for an end to all cultural-exchange programs; they were simply "a Communist confidence game."[36] The captive nations should be "encourag[ed] to overthrow their captors."[37] Should a revolt occur inside Red China, "we should encourage South Koreans and the South Vietnamese to join Free Chinese forces in a combined effort to liberate the enslaved peoples of Asia."[38] As a matter of moral principle, the Arizonian wrote, "we should withdraw diplomatic recognition from all Communist governments, including that of the Soviet Union, thereby serving notice on the world that we regard such governments as neither legitimate nor permanent."[39]

Such was the tone of early conservatism in its foreign-policy statements. Translated into day-to-day commentary in the pages of *National Review,* it resulted in such firm positions as that expressed in the famous Hungary Pledge adopted by the American Friends of the Captive Nations, which received the magazine's warm endorsement. It stated:

> The Soviet regime having by the Hungarian massacre demonstrated once again its isolation from the moral community, I pledge that until all Soviet troops and police are withdrawn from Hungary, I will enter into no economic, social, political or cultural relations with that regime . . . or with any persons or institutions freely condoning the Hungarian massacre. . . .

In fact, *National Review* found the pledge not quite strong enough. The editors felt constrained to add that it did not "precommit them in any way to a softened view of Soviet Communism even should the troops be withdrawn from Hungary."[40]

In the same issue in which the pledge appeared (December 8, 1956), there was another editorial that lashed out at the Eisenhower administration for joining in the U.N. General Assembly resolution of November 24, 1956 condemning Britain, France, and Israel for failing to withdraw forthwith from conquered Egyptian territory in the aftermath of the Suez war. In a mood that epitomized the approach of fifties conservatism they declared:

> . . . the historical meaning of the United States vote on the "Afro-Asian resolution" emerges: *Over the humiliated forms of our two oldest and closest allies, we clasp the hands of the murderers of the Christian heroes of Hungary** as we run in shameless and vain pursuit of the "good will" of Asia and Africa's teeming pagan multitudes . . .
>
> . . . Can we suppose that the alien cultures of Asia will prove allies more dependable than the Christian nations of Europe? . . .[41]

What should have been the American reaction to the plight of the "Christian heroes of Hungary"? Fifties conservatives believed, as Goldwater put it in *The Conscience,* that in a situation such as occurred in Budapest in 1956

*Italics are *NR*'s

. . . we ought to present the Kremlin with an ultimatum forbidding Soviet intervention, and be prepared, if the ultimatum
is rejected, to move a highly mobile task force equipped with
appropriate nuclear weapons to the scene of the revolt. . . . An
actual clash . . . would be unlikely; the mere threat of American intervention, coupled with the Kremlin's knowledge that
the fighting would occur amid a hostile population and could
easily spread . . . would probably result in Soviet acceptance
of the ultimatum.[42]

Having failed to respond this way, the editors of *National
Review* thought, the only decent thing for America to do

would be to break off diplomatic relations with the aggressor
government and its puppet and to move at once for their expul-
sion from the U.N. . . .[43]

In general, *National Review* believed, in the words of a 1957
editorial, that one of the prime goals of United States foreign policy
in relation to Russia should be "To Keep the Pot Boiling." *NR*
exclaimed:

How irrational and absurd, then, the frantic Western eager-
ness to "relax tensions"! Should we not, rather, tighten every
tension that can exacerbate the Kremlin's inner conflicts? How
absurd, by a T.V. screen or a disarmament offer or a "summit
conference," to build up the prestige of a Communist chief.
. . . If we were rational, would we not rather give our careful
concern today to moves that would deflate and denigrate
Khrushchev and Zhukov, hold them up to embarrassment,
ridicule and scorn? . . .[44]

Today, the clear, moralistically phrased policies of fifties conservatism have gone the way of the dodo. In their place American
rightists have turned to a bland, neo-Metternichean policy of "two-
way-street detente" and "containment"—which in reality is the
same policy that was advanced by the fifties liberals whom the "old
conservatives" found incapable of defending Western civilization
some twenty years ago.

The retreat had already begun in the early sixties. William F.
Buckley, Jr. in a *National Review* article in 1964 sought to explain
away the hard-line views of then presidential-primary candidate
Goldwater. He wrote that when Goldwater spoke of "victory" over

23

the Soviet Union he only meant it in the sense of frustrating the Soviets' declared ambition "to bury us." As for liberation of the captive nations, Buckley explained that all Goldwater wanted was their "ultimate liberation. . . . It is not likely that we can effect their liberation in the immediate future."

Buckley's moderating words stand in stark contrast to Goldwater's stated "Objective" of United States foreign policy, namely, "the disintegration of the Soviet empire." As for the satellite countries, Goldwater, when writing in *National Review* in March of 1961, did not seem quite as patient as did Buckley three years later. He said:

> [Our policy on Eastern Europe must] begin by having serious designs on it . . . American policy must be geared to the offensive. Our appetite for Communist territory must be just as keen as theirs for non-Communist territory. Our efforts to extend freedom behind the Iron Curtain must be no less vigorous than their never-ending campaign to spread the influence of Communism in the free world.
>
> We should encourage the captive peoples to revolt against their Communist rulers. . . .
>
> We must ourselves be prepared to undertake military operations against vulnerable Communist regimes. . . .[45]

The metamorphosis of James Burnham's foreign-policy views serves to illustrate the general erosion of the once firmly held principles of fifties conservatives. Burnham, whom Nash describes as having provided the "theoretical formulation" of the "militant, global anti-Communism" of the early Right, seems to have evolved from an "evangelistic"[46] rhetoric of liberation to a policy of containment and coexistence. Thus, in 1947, he wrote that our foreign relations with the Communists will never be settled until "the present Soviet regime is overthrown, and world Communism as a whole rendered impotent."[47] Likewise in 1953, Burnham still believed that "liberation is the only defense against a Soviet world victory."[48] By 1957, though, the former advocate of establishing counterrevolutionary military units to liberate Eastern Europe had decided to throw in the towel, signifying the end of round one of his ideological retreat. Bemoaning the "rhetorical intransigence" of "hard anti-Communists" for whom "it is more congenial to sit undisturbed" in their "vague" denunciations of "the 1949–56 stabilization," he called for a "withdrawal of all occupation [foreign]

24

troops from all of Central and Eastern Europe" and "military neutralization of the entire area."[49] By 1964 Burnham had gone a bit
further. No longer was the overthrow of the Soviet government, or
even the neutralization of Europe, to be the goal of our foreign
policy, only the "reduction of the power of the Communist enterprise." How much reduction? Only as much as necessary to make
it impossible for the Soviets to "threaten the security of America."
Finally, by 1972 Burnham had, according to Nash, opted for a
moderate "balance of power strategy." Gone from his columns in
National Review was all talk of liberation, victory, heightening of
tensions, or overthrow of the Soviet regime. Instead, the author of
The Coming Defeat of Communism (1950) was urging that we
attempt to "open up" Soviet society somewhat by asking for internal political changes in the Russian system in return for increased
U.S. trade. The result of this would be "the most promising of
auguries for both peace and decency."[50] Burnham had come a long
way from 1947, when he called "the defeat and annihilation" of the
United States "probable"[51] unless we pursued a policy of victory.

As if to seal the abdication of the victory theme, the 1976 presidential hopeful of the American Right, Governor Ronald Reagan of
California, limited his proposals on foreign affairs basically to fifties liberal containment coupled with some hard-sounding noises.
In his 1968 book *The Creative Society* Reagan wrote that the goal
of American policy in Vietnam must be "victory." The "victory" of
which Reagan spoke was, however, vastly different from the
"liberation" or "disintegration of Communism" envisioned in the
fifties. One relevant passage in a chapter with the tough-sounding
title "What Price Peace?" goes as follows:

> The war in Vietnam must be fought through to victory,
> meaning first, an end to North Vietnamese aggression, and
> second, an honorable and safe peace for our South Vietnam
> friends.[52]

The goal of Reagan's foreign policy was not Goldwater's old
"Objective" of winning the war against Communism. The former
California governor summed it up as follows:

> Our policy should be . . . that we are going to supply and
> encourage people in other nations who are not communists,
> and that we'll use our technological might to keep those na-

tions free. The ultimate of all this defense will be that: the Soviet Union and other communist nations will realize that they cannot destroy freedom in the world. . . .[53]

Truman, Stevenson, Acheson, Rusk, and McNamara could easily have lived with such a policy. At this point it is largely unnecessary, I believe, to document the gradual conservative acquiescence on other issues, once considered essential, like welfare statism, internal security, taxation, and a host of other concerns. Only the remnant of "extreme" rightists has clung to the classic positions of fifties conservatism.

Let us now consider the various detrimental effects that this retreat has had on the political fortunes of the American Right. In order for conservatism—or any other political doctrine—to remain viable, it must stand for certain specific things, or at the very least create various *impressions* to which the public can relate. Now, Anglo-Saxon politics tends to be conducted in somewhat vaguer terms than the politics of continental Europe, especially of the Latin countries. Despite its subdued character, though, there is still a historically demonstrable need, even in the English political tradition, for a comprehensibly articulated public philosophy. Having abandoned its basic positions, American conservatism no longer represents a clear body of doctrine. As the European conservative Erik von Kuehnelt-Leddihn has observed, what the American Right needs at the moment is a "blueprint" that is "concrete, magnetic, [and] dynamic."[54] These sentiments have been echoed by the American political analyst Kevin Phillips, who has called for conservatives to devise "positive approaches to housing, education, unemployment, productivity, and the rest of our national challenges."[55]

It can safely be said that until such time as fifties conservatism can be revived (a highly unlikely prospect), or an equally forceful and energetic program offered in its place, the right wing in America will be unable to present itself as a distinct and attractive movement to the American people. A simple defense of the basic institutions of Anglo-Saxon liberty, to which Buckley summoned the "new conservatives" in 1969, will not be enough to demonstrate the necessity of a *separate* conservative cause. As a matter of fact, it was precisely for this "sin" of failing to spell out a clear-cut conservatism that would contrast starkly with the doctrines of liberalism that the mainstream conservatives in the fifties had anathema-

26

tized the rightism of such men as Peter Viereck and Clinton Rossiter. Any sort of conservative revival in America must be preceded by a reformulation of conservatism as a political entity with an important message for the seventies and beyond.

The virtual evaporation of clear working notions of conservatism has had a second damaging effect: it has broken down the old allegiances of hard-core conservatives and shattered their united front. In recent years we have witnessed the once undisputed political leaders of the American Right seemingly selling their souls to the forces of what they once bitingly described as "me-too Republicanism." In 1968, 1972, and especially 1976 the foremost political spokesmen of the movement, men like Senator Carl Curtis of Nebraska, Senator Strom Thurmond of South Carolina, and the previously mentioned Senators Goldwater and Tower, supported the vapid, pragmatic, middle-of-the-road emptiness of Presidents Nixon and Ford. In an apparent repudiation of everything they had fought so hard for in the Republican Party for so many years, the conservative elite of the GOP backed Nixon over Governor Reagan in 1968, thereby sabotaging any hopes the former actor had for the nomination that year. Again in 1972, when Congressman John Ashbrook of Ohio launched a courageous, and probably career-destructive, symbolic challenge to President Nixon, the top-name conservatives ignored the opportunity to popularize conservative opposition to Nixon's obviously leftward course— wage-price controls, appeasement of Red China, SALT accords, and many other things. Ashbrook was left to struggle virtually alone as the Goldwaters and Towers remained loyal to Nixon. Goldwater and Tower finally relinquished the mantle of conservative leadership in 1976 when both men, at times stooping to the same rhetorical low blows that their opponents had used against them in the early sixties, assailed Governor Reagan's bid to deprive Ford of the Republican nomination. It is quite conceivable, indeed, that given the slim margin by which Ford eventually triumphed at the Kansas City convention, the opposition of Goldwater, Tower, and Curtis actually caused the Californian's defeat.[56] The shock and surprise of conservatives at the desertion of the leadership ("Et tu, Barry?" was the *Human Events* headline) were magnified when, amazingly, the former Mr. Conservative began attacking Reagan for advocating positions that Goldwater himself had warmly espoused in the early sixties!

A few leading conservative intellectuals loudly bemoaned Goldwater as a Benedict Arnold. William Rusher, the publisher of *National Review,* suggested that "Goldwater's grip on conservative principles just isn't (*and perhaps never was*)* the absolutely dependable thing we believed it to be."[57] In my opinion, however, Goldwater's weird statements during the 1976 campaign—about Reagan's "dangerous frame of mind," Rockefeller's potential to be "a damn good president," and Ford's conservatism ("indistinguishable from Reagan's")—were the direct result of the failure of rightist intellectuals to stand firm and man the dikes against the tide of events in the sixties. By abandoning in their books and periodicals nearly everything that Goldwaterism had once represented, the conservative thinkers enabled the 1964 GOP nominee tacitly to surrender his position of leadership in the movement. As any perceptive person could have easily seen even in the early sixties, Goldwater was never an especially profound thinker. To answer Rusher's query, the Arizonan's grip on his principles was probably no worse than that of the average politician in a universal-suffrage democracy. He was merely the spokesman and, above all, the symbolic representation of fifties conservatism. As the theoreticians of that conservatism began to forsake its tenets, Goldwater no longer found any reason to continue to champion a cause that clearly (to paraphrase Karl Hess) would *never* triumph.

To illustrate the erosion of conservative Republican opposition to the middle-of-the-road-ism of so-called moderates in their party, we need only look back to April 8, 1957, when the freshman senator from Arizona, Barry Goldwater, rose in a near-empty Senate chamber to deliver a lengthy attack on the liberal economic policies of the Eisenhower administration. Lashing out at the "fiscal irresponsibility [of] this Republican administration," calling it "a betrayal of the people's trust," the man who was soon to be cast as Mr. Conservative denounced

> the faulty premises of "Modern Republicanism," [which is a] splinterized concept of Republican philosophy . . . [a] strange and mysterious force seems to have descended upon Republicans.[58]

In reality, Goldwater's censure of Eisenhower Republicanism merely gave political voice to the intellectual elite of the Right,

*Italics are Rusher's.

which at that time had not yet progressed to an acceptance of "mainstream Republicans." When Eisenhower left office in 1961, *National Review*, for one, bid him good riddance. Describing the general as "the goodhearted man providence inflicted on the West," the editors of *NR* summarized his foreign and domestic policies in a manner and style typical of early sixties conservatism:

> The Communists had the measure of Dwight Eisenhower.
> . . . It was Dwight Eisenhower who concluded in Korea . . .
> a strategically indefensible treaty . . . who stood by while
> Red China consolidated its hold on the wretched masses of
> Asia . . . who instituted those pernicious circumlocutions that
> go by the name of "cultural" and "economic" exchange . . .
> who invited Khrushchev to come over here and to test, at first
> hand, the moral idiocy of the West . . .
> . . . When the time came to defend ourselves against those
> who would push us further toward Socialism, all we had to
> offer was the mechanical reincarnation of Mr. Eisenhower's
> Progressive Moderation, Richard Nixon. Oh Lord!
> . . . We pray [Eisenhower] will never realize what a total,
> desperate failure he was, compared with what he might have
> been.[59]

Today, of course, neither *National Review* nor any other self-respecting rightist publication would ever print an equivalent condemnation of the Nixon or Ford administrations, for the simple reason that respectable conservatism no longer possesses the vitality and firmness that a strong grasp of basic principles, together with starkly advanced programs, automatically results in. Accordingly, when *National Review* in 1961 lashed out at the half-hearted Eisenhower-Nixon resistance to the "forces that gnaw at the strength of our country . . . the bureaucratic parasites, the labor union monopolists, the centralizers," deriding it for being "so theoretically anemic as to leave us disarmed," conservative politicians such as Goldwater followed suit in the political forum. Today, despite the obvious fact that the Nixon-Ford opposition to bureaucracy, Big Labor, Communism, and the like is just as "theoretically anemic" as was Eisenhower's, *National Review* no longer editorializes about it. Apparently, the Eisenhower anemia was contagious. As Donald Atwell Zoll wrote in 1974:

> . . . the mood of conservatism has perceptibly changed . . . it
> has lost much of its compelling grandeur, its elemental sense

of passion. . . . It has, in contrast, become increasingly pros-
perous (in a comparative sense), respectable . . . cautious and,
if you will forgive, fat—the antithesis of that almost classical
leanness characteristic of conservative thought and writing in
those recent eras when conservatism felt itself on the verge of
being swept away and with it the civilization it had sought to
maintain.[60]

"Contemporary conservatism," continues Zoll, "lacks the crys-
talline hardness" that would enable it to hammer out a philosophy
and resultant programs and positions as it once did. L. Brent Bozell
saw this tendency toward doctrinal retreat among conservatives as
early as 1969. In his open letter addressed to the conservative
movement (see page 14) he suggested the underlying reason behind
the decision of leading conservatives to support Nixon over Reagan
in 1968:

> Reagan . . . was the obvious heir . . . of Goldwater and the
> conservative program. . . . You neglected him because Nixon
> was early in the field, had initiative, momentum; to push
> Reagan in the circumstances would have required the kind of
> energy that carried the day in San Francisco. But you no
> longer had much energy, which is a function of will, which in
> turn is a function of conviction. . . .[61]

Seen in this light, was not Goldwater's startling animosity to
Reagan more the *result* of the views of conservative intellectuals
than a denial of them? The titular head of the conservative movement was never more than the sum of the parts of rightism as
articulated by its thinkers. As the thinkers themselves led the
movement into a posture of drift and vagueness, the Arizona senator could quite logically conclude that Nixon and Ford were true
representatives of the "new conservatism."

So, too, the confusion of rightist principles has led to a break-
down of unity among American conservatives, with various feud-
ing factions making their appearance. For convenience sake, let us
call them the "true believers," "the soft-liners," and "the remnant." The "true believers" belong to such groups as Young Americans for Freedom and the American Conservative Union.[62] These
groups seem totally unaware of the rightist abandonment of fifties
conservatism. Disregarding the obvious fact that their conservatism (which in reality advocates nothing more than "containment"

abroad and modified welfarism at home) is to all intents and purposes the equivalent of the liberalism of the late forties and fifties, they serenely view themselves as the only true keepers of the tablets and are surprised and hurt when their reformed conservatism is not universally accepted by conservative politicians, or by pure libertarians (who took the laissez-faire of fifties conservatism literally), or by pure metaphysical conservatives (who took the anti-Communism of fifties conservatism literally), or by pure constitutionalists (who took the strict-construction doctrines of fifties conservatism literally). These "true believers" have come a long way, to judge from what George Nash says in his intellectual history of the movement:

> In the 1960s [the conservative] revolt against the state began to seem less . . . doctrinaire.[63]
>
> * * *
>
> . . . a subtle change [occurred] in the conservative foreign policy of the early 1970s . . . conservative foreign policy more and more came to resemble the old liberal policy of containment.[64]

If, as Nash points out, fifties liberalism and seventies conservatism are identical in many respects,[65] may we not conclude that the "true believers" equate the true expression of the political Right with whatever that expression happens to be at any given historical moment? "True believer" conservatism extends its *nihil obstat* at different times to thinkers ranging from such fifties favorites as Willi Schlamm, Medford Evans, E. Merrill Root, and Revilo P. Oliver to such seventies luminaries as Walt W. Rostow, Dean Acheson, Nathan Glazer, and Norman Podhoretz. In sum, then, the "true believer" is not dedicated to conservatism as a matter of principle but essentially as an expression of nondoctrinal party loyalty. Whatever programs happen to be identified publicly as conservative he will seize upon and call his own. With the exclusionary zeal of party loyalists, the "true believers," despite their increasingly vague program, have sought to shut out of their ranks any and all dissidents who fail to toe their line. And they have largely succeeded.

The "soft-liners" are rightists who have come to feel that fifties conservatism was a purist, utopian movement that inevitably mellowed as it began to experience the realities of political and intellectual life. Unlike the "true believers," the "soft-liners" readily admit the existence of this evolutionary process and welcome it. They continue to regard themselves as conservatives. Indeed, they see their moderate conservatism as the true maturation of the American Right. A fitting representative of this school of thought would perhaps be Ralph de Toledano, who advocated conservative support for the Richard Nixon type of Republican long before it became fashionable to do so among the *National Review* group. This "soft-line" conservatism fits in easily with Goldwater and Tower's current position, which favors "moderate" Republicans as opposed to conservatives.

The "remnant" is generally not talked about by mainstream conservatives.[66] *National Review* read the "remnant" out of the movement in 1965[67] and George Nash sweeps it out of *The Conservative Intellectual Movement in America* with two short sentences in his introduction.[68] The "remnant" includes the John Birch Society, the Conservative Society of America, the Christian Crusade, and (on a far more reasoned, but no less doctrinally pure level) the ever-struggling Americans for Constitutional Action. For all its excesses (and these, of course, seem much greater today than they did in the fifties because of the leftward movement of mainstream conservatism since then), which generally center on some sort of conspiratorial view of recent history,[69] the "remnant" remains just that: a remnant of conservatives who still advocate victory over Communism[70] and support both laissez-faire and doctrinaire constitutionalism.

The inability of conservatives to agree, in Eliseo Vivas' words, on "some working notion as to which of our values are basic and which are not" has resulted in all sorts of internecine warfare between competing conservative groups. On the one hand, the "remnant" (ever given to absurdities) regards the centrists as at best dupes of "The Conspiracy" and at worst its conscious agents. On the other hand, the "true believers" have written the "soft-liners" out of the movement ("Goldwater and Tower, Exit Stage Left" headlined YAF's *New Guard* on its June 1976 cover) and consigned the "remnant" to, in Russell Kirk's words, "the lunatic fringe." Finally, the "soft-liners," with little conservatism left to speak of, have joined the ranks of the mindless pragmatism of the Eisenhower-Nixon-Ford triumvirate and look upon other conservatives as "extremists": e.g., Goldwater speaking of Reagan.

The third damaging effect that the increasing haziness of American conservatism has had in recent years has been in relation to the "new" or, alternatively, emerging Republican majority of traditionally minded Americans. Basically, the thesis of New Majority advocates like Kevin Phillips and William Rusher is that (1) the Sun Belt of America, that is, the South and the West and to a lesser degree the Plains states, has become a bastion of conservative strength, and (2) the middle to lower-middle and even lower class white, big-city ethnics, as well as their somewhat more affluent suburban counterparts, are ready to embrace traditionalist conservatism. The theory optimistically continues to say that by some amalgamation of patriotism, conservative morality, strong foreign policy, religiosity, and (here is the hitch!) economic activism, presto, there appears an overwhelming electoral majority guaranteed to sweep the nation. The thesis is alluring and resembles in many respects both the European rightist strategy (in both its monarchial and nationalist incarnations) and the traditionalist-populist battle plan that we in America associate with the William Jennings Bryan campaign of 1896 and the Union Party effort of William Lemke in 1936. In a crude way the American Party in its George Wallace days[71] also attempted to forge such a coalition.

Now, if the Right had some clearly articulated first principles, and programs derived from such principles, it would be a great deal easier to evaluate the proposed new coalition. Conservatives could subject the political policies that the alignment calls for to a searching critique and determine whether they can be reconciled with "essential" conservatism.

Instead, conservatism drifts along on its fragmented course. The "remnant" continues to advance the case of fifties conservatism and, thanks to its own further fragmentation, offered *two* microscopic minor parties to the American voter in 1976, the American Party and the American Independent Party. The "remnant" remains true to its doctrinally pure self and prepares itself (in the true spirit of fifties conservatism) to go down with the sinking wreck of Western civilization. For the likes of Tom Anderson and Lester Maddox,[72] the New Majority philosophy is a heretical conservatism to which they pay no attention.

The "true believers," despite their quiet recognition of the fact that their rhetoric of "severely limited government . . . appears to be electorally vulnerable,"[73] as *National Review* recently acknowledged editorially, and that "people today . . . expect an activist economic policy," as Jeffrey Hart has written, still seem determined to run the movement like a closed church. They not only exclude from their ranks their natural allies, the "soft-liners" and the "remnant," but by conveying the image of McKinley-Hoover Republicanism—looking, in Hart's words, "as if they just stepped out of a corporate board room"—and by exuding "a rote hostility to organized labor,"[74] they have cut themselves off from the second part of the New Majority, the white ethnics. This became especially evident in 1976 when the Reagan campaign all but ignored the urban industrial states populated by blue-collar conservatives, such as New York, Pennsylvania, New Jersey, and Ohio. In so doing the Reagan people turned their backs on the advice of the chief theoretician of the New Majority, William Rusher, who holds that the new coalition must appeal to a broader base by "moderat[ing] the near-Puritan severity of traditional conservative economics" in the spirit of the early papal social encyclicals[75] (*Rerum Novarum, Quadragesimo Anno,* etc.) and by affirming clearly that it is the government's responsibility "that no one in the country ever need go without adequate food, clothing, shelter, or medical care."[76] Perhaps, as *National Review* suggested, Reagan's choice of Senator Schweiker for vice-president was a tacit admission of these realities. It did not appear so, however, for just a few moments after Reagan had lost the nomination, John Sears, his campaign manager, declared in a national television interview that the Reagan effort had not been "ideological," but had been undertaken merely to demonstrate the superior personal virtues of the California governor! Since Sears reportedly conceived of the Schweiker gambit, it is unlikely that this young pragmatist was cognizant of any deeper issues when he chose the Pennsylvania senator.

At this point it may appear that my analysis contradicts itself. I have been lambasting my fellow rightists in the form of two seemingly contradictory critiques. I first attacked their surrender of basic principles and now I accuse them of not surrendering enough of those principles to woo the New Majority. To clear up this objection, I wish to underscore that I have not yet discussed the relative merits of the various planks of fifties conservatism or, for that matter, of the New Majority philosophy. For the moment, all that is necessary is that these two points be made: (1) that conservatives have fumbled the opportunity to recast the movement in an attractive package that could appeal to the various groups of the New Majority, and (2) that fifties conservatism is dead and has not bequeathed to the American Right a legitimate successor.

It would seem that as conservatives contemplate their long retreat of the past twenty years, they would be prompted to search out and reexamine their own philosophical foundations. If conservatism is not what it was claimed to be in the fifties, then *what, precisely, is it*? If the American Right today would view with surprise its own positions of the fifties, then how would it appraise its stances of the 1920s or 1890s?[77] Is conservatism nothing more than the reflective conscience of triumphant liberalism? Is the philosophy of the Right irresistibly swept along in a stream of constantly evolving positions?[78]

Rightists in America must return to their basic premises and ask themselves what in the movement is permanent. Russell Kirk comes close to fingering the problem when he writes:

> By and large, radical thinkers have won the day. For a century and a half, conservatives have yielded ground in a manner which, except for occasionally successful rear-guard actions, must be described as a rout.[79]

Alas, Kirk neglects the central philosophical problem: Are conservatives at all interested, either practically or theoretically, in regaining the ground they have given up? Thomas Molnar puts things in somewhat clearer perspective when he says:

> Through 1789, 1917, and 1945 the "substance of inner life," as Salazar put it, evaporated, although after each date some, always fewer, old forms still survived, creating the impression that the loss is tolerable. Thus after each turning point, the domain of what the counter-revolutionaries considered as *essential* diminished, while increasingly more had to be jettisoned as *inessential*.[80]

Although Molnar goes on to say that these changes are not philosophical but "enforced by necessity," it is by no means obvious that such is the case in the long run. For example, the gradual abandonment by American conservatives of the theme of opposition to democracy, while pragmatic when it began, has become essentially philosophical. As the "pro-republic, anti-democracy" forces in America lost, in 1800 to the Jeffersonian Democrats, in the 1820s to the forces of Jacksonian democracy, in the teens of this century to the proponents of popular senatorial elections, in the 1920s to the women's-suffrage movement, and in the 1960s to the

35

anti-poll-tax contingent, they seemed to adopt the positions of their previous opponents and to incorporate them into their own ideological baggage. One can think of no conservative politician today who would not regard all the leftist-originated elements of our system as part and parcel of American democracy.

In sum, the American Right is confronted with two deeply significant questions, which go to its very raison d'être. First, what is the real meaning (if any) of American conservatism, now that it has given up its attachment to laissez-faire, strict construction, and victory over Communism, just as earlier generations of American rightists dropped their doctrines of theocracy (the Puritan-Pilgrim stage of Cotton Mather, John Winthrop, John Cotton, etc.), a strong elitist federal government (the early Federalist stage of Alexander Hamilton, Fisher Ames, John Marshall, etc.), antidemocracy (the anti-Jackson stage of Daniel Webster, Joseph Story, James Kent, etc.), states' rights (the Southern resistance of John Randolph, John Calhoun, John Taylor, etc.), the Protestant work ethic (the extreme laissez-faire of William Graham Sumner, Justice Stephen Field, Justice George Sutherland, etc.), anti-Catholic Republicanism (the "Rum, Romanism, and Rebellion" stage of James Blaine, Rutherford Hayes, and Elihu Root, etc.), manifest destiny (the imperialist stage of Josiah Strong, Alfred Mahan, and Henry Cabot Lodge, Sr., etc.), and neutrality in foreign affairs (the isolationist stage of Charles Lindbergh, John T. Flynn, and Oswald Garrison Villard, etc.). Second, what in the final analysis is the essence (if any) of conservatism, if its public stance can change with such amazing rapidity? Briefly, is there any real meaning to conservatism in general and to American conservatism in particular?

If the answer to these questions is that conservatism does have meaning (and I hope to elucidate exactly what that meaning is in later chapters), then the natural result will be that rightists must express their intellectual underpinnings in *coherent* and *positive* terminology. It will not suffice for them simply to battle against those who would exile God from the cosmos and substitute the valueless, relativist, subjectivist universe of the amoral enemies of mankind. This task is, of course, important and is best represented by the work of the late Leo Strauss. Similarly, it will not be enough for conservatives to war against those who would make God immanent in man and substitute the gnostic, magical ideologies of Communists, Comtean positivists, and the like for reality as we see it.

36

Eric Voegelin[81] has carried the conservative case on these matters to the public. The success of these undertakings, while basic to any conservative victory plan, will not be enough to construct a clear conservative alternative to these diabolical systems. This does not mean that conservatives must construct political "final solutions" to the problems of mankind à la the Left. On the contrary, it is my view (more on this later) that a program of practical politics is secondary to the real chore of the political Right, which is to understand its own theoretical foundations and to package them attractively.

However, we are getting somewhat ahead of ourselves. For the present we can clearly see that the task that lies before us is to understand the inner reality of conservatism and to seek to express that reality in terms that can be politically advantageous in the seventies. Thus, Chapter 2 will be an attempt to point out the underlying unity in the seemingly diametrically opposed philosophies of metaphysical conservatives, empirical conservatives, and historical conservatives. I hope to arrive at a definition of conservatism broad enough to embrace a metaphysical conservative like Donoso Cortes, an empirical conservative like David Hume, and a historical conservative like Edmund Burke. (In contemporary terms this would mean showing the essential agreement between a Frederick Wilhelmsen, a Donald Zoll, and a Russell Kirk, for example.) The third chapter will examine how the basic principles of conservatism were symbolized in America at various times and in sometimes contradictory political forms, while remaining true to the central essence. Chapter 4 will look at the reasons for the failure of the American Right to win popular support in post-1932 America. Contrasting with this recent inability of conservatives to advance their case successfully will be the bright outlook for the Right if it can develop a new form of popular expression that draws on the experience of European conservatives, who have in some respects achieved greater success than American conservatives in the twentieth century.[82] This will be covered in the fifth chapter, where I will raise the prospect that conservatism could become a dominant force in America if it learns to appeal to Sun Belters, Southerners, and the white middle- and lower-class labor forces. In Chapter 6 I will weigh the chances for such a renewal and offer some practical suggestions.

Conservatives, the determined defenders of Judeo-Christian Western civilization and the bearers of the empirical truths of the human condition, have been fleeing in defeat from battle after battle with the twin heresies of mankind, namely, relativism and ideology. This flight, which began in the eighteenth century, has become vastly more desperate of late. Many perceptive rightists have expressed concern over the lateness of the hour. John Hallowell believes we are currently living through the "last pains of a dying Western civilization."[83] Erik von Kuehnelt-Leddihn views the failure of the Right as so complete that the "Western world moves nearer and nearer to the abyss"[84] and except for "a few straws in the wind" there is "little ground for hope."[85] Thomas Molnar has described the situation in stark terms. He wrote in his book *The Counter-Revolution:*

> To sum it up, the relentless and organized revolutionary assault has finally reached the United States as the embodiment of the pre-1789 political order, and the church, as the embodiment of the transcendental order. Our civilization will no doubt come to an end the day the Catholic Church and the United States join the revolution.[86]

America at present appears to have very little understanding of its all-important role. Even Rome has of late been sending out increasingly upsetting signals that it, too, no longer has a clear grasp of its historical mission in the world. If the eternal values and revelatory truths of Western civilization are to command the loyalty of more than a small remnant of modern men, conservatives must give force, coherence, and energy to their program. They can do so by vigorously defending, without recourse to half-hearted compromise, the truths of traditional faith, while seeking to understand—and answer—the questions put forth by an extremely man-centered age. In the ensuing pages I hope to lay the groundwork for such an endeavor, in the hope that the "camp of the saints" will never be surrounded.

2 What Is Conservatism?

The epoch-making historical circumstances of the past two hundred years have created the impression that conservatism is by its very nature a negative persuasion. This popular misconception has been fed by the constant tendency of rightists to wage a *defensive* struggle against the various leftist forces of the modern era. However, conservatism is not by nature a negative mode of thought. As rightist setbacks have multiplied in recent centuries, conservatives have invariably been forced to think, speak, and act defensively. Should conservatives succeed in halting and eventually reversing the swift-flowing leftist current of modern times, thus gaining an opportunity to exhibit their intellectual and practical wares at leisure to the public, then we can be assured that this situation will change. Conservatism would undoubtedly, under such favorable conditions, garb itself in a wide variety of original and constructive forms just as it did in earlier historical periods. For the time being, though, as the Left continues to vanquish the forces allied against it on almost every major battleground—indeed, in almost every minor skirmish—conservatives are continually obliged to play the role of what appears to be a defeated remnant of perpetual naysayers.

But there is a hidden blessing for the Right in this posture of dissent. It has prompted conservative thinkers over the past two hundred years or so to seek to formulate clearly the philosophical underpinnings of their political, social, and religious theories. That conservatives are willing to engage in self-appraisal is of course due in no small measure to the unfortunate straits in which the right wing has found itself in recent history. There is much more Monday morning quarterbacking in the skull sessions of the defeated than in those of the victors. In contrast to their ancestors in pre-Enlightenment Europe, where the philosophical first principles of what was eventually to become the *ancien régime* were pretty much taken for granted, the post-1789 restorers of the old order were forced to reexamine their fundamentals in order to articulate their position in the hostile surroundings of leftist-dominated societies. To illustrate this we need only refer to the example of Russian conservative theory under the czars. Because of imperial Russia's seeming immunity to the proverbial sneeze that Paris gave on July 14, 1789, the Russian Right was never called upon to meditate its reason for existence. Accordingly, Russian conservatism was in all probability the most underdeveloped school of rightism in continental Europe. Adversity inevitably tends either to destroy a theory or, alternatively, to refine and strengthen it. When the once widely held conservative beliefs about religion, political theory, and the like were questioned on a large scale, the result was that they were either defeated or purified by fire. The past two hundred years, then, have seen a large amount of profound intellectual activity by thinkers of the Right.

Despite some doctrinal haziness of late, which I have discussed in Chapter 1, the resurgent American conservative movement of the post–World War II period has also shown a distinct interest in probing its own rationale for existence. By contrast, the contemporary American Left, with the smug complacency of the successful, takes its own theoretical assumptions for granted: egalitarianism, the innate goodness of man, and the infinite plasticity of human nature. As Jeffrey Hart once pointed out,

> conservative intellectuals . . . are willing to debate first principles. (When was the last time first principles were debated in the pages of the *New Republic* or the *Nation*?) The liberals would seem to have agreed for so long on their assumptions that they have forgotten what they are.[1]

One of the manifestations of this rigorous self-analysis to which rightists have subjected themselves is the frequent attempt by some leading conservative thinker to define the precise "essence," "nature," "meaning," and so on of conservatism. Over the years many popular conservative thinkers have put forth their ideas on what the credo of the Right does, or else should, consist of. On the whole these efforts have not succeeded. They have failed to unify rightist intellectuals or to excite the fancy of the conservative rank-and-file. Despite their occasional unity in the practical arena, conservatives find themselves unable to come to terms with one another in the theoretical drawing room. Thus, it would appear at the outset that conservatives are doomed to pursue a course of improvisational activism without recourse to first principles, or at best to feel with Peter Viereck that conservatism "is not science, but art."*

In line with Viereck's desire to reduce conservatism to "[a] balancing and harmonizing . . . [a] transcending of isms"[2] is the question raised, or if it is not raised, at least it is sensed by many American rightists: Do we really *need* a "philosophy of conservatism"? The reasoning of this group is that it would be far better for rightists to concentrate their energies on activism—on attractively packaging their program for the public. Now, I readily grant that American conservatives must seek out more creative and appealing methods of carrying their case to the nation. I heartily endorse the idea. But all the activism in the world cannot do away with the need to formulate some suitable definition of conservatism. On the contrary, it is my contention that the development and clarification of conservative theory are ultimately the *only* means of reviving the sagging political fortunes of American conservatism.

*Of course, Viereck is right to a certain extent. Conservatism is not a "science" in the sense of being a final solution, an ideological cure-all for mankind's woes. As I hope to show later, however, it is a great deal more than an "art." Actually, Viereck himself, with his crusading antitotalitarianism, his distinct brand of extremely humanistic and moralistic conservatism, and his philosophic commitment to pluralism and tolerance, is far from being a mere "artist." Instead, he seems to have very definite ideas about what conservatism is and how to translate this meaning into practical politics.

By the way, now that *National Review* has made its peace with both the welfare state and containment foreign policy, isn't it time that it took the works of Viereck and Clinton Rossiter off the *Index* of mainstream conservatism? After all, these men's supposed sins had never been on the level of conservative theory. They had read their Burke and Metternich well, but their fault was merely their rejection of McKinley-Hoover Republicanism. By adopting such a position they simply outdistanced the *NR* group by about fifteen years.

In the previous chapter the abandonment of fifties conservatism and its adverse effects on the Right were noted. Let us now turn to a related theme, the necessity of providing a working doctrinal framework for conservatism and the impossibility of engaging in any form of sustained political or social activism without one. Consider for a moment the conservative attitude toward the welfare state. This is an area where the failure of the American Right to return to the philosophical locker room and hold some tough skull sessions has taken an immense toll politically.

In the fifties the American rightist position on the welfare state was expressed clearly, but was carelessly sustained from a theoretical standpoint. The position, as spelled out in the "Credenda" of *National Review*'s maiden issue, was:

> It is the job of centralized government (in peacetime) to protect its citizens' lives, liberty and property. All other activities tend to diminish freedom and hamper progress. The growth of government—the dominant social feature of this century—must be fought relentlessly.[3]

Translated into practical terms, this meant that, as Frank Meyer expressed it in 1959:

> The conservative believes . . . that the New Deal represents the breakthrough of socialism and that only by its reversal can a free society in America be guaranteed.[4]

As I pointed out in the first chapter, conservatives today have traveled a long way from the doctrinaire antistatism of the fifties. In 1972 Jeffrey Hart admitted as much when he wrote:

> Conservative criticism of one or another welfare scheme . . . has, as a matter of fact, been based not so much on ideology as on the argument that the specific scheme . . . will not produce the results desired . . .[5]

Our concern at the moment, however, is not to document yet another example of the great retreat of the American Right. Instead, let us take a look at the nature of the apologetics that conservatives have offered over the past century to support their free-market position. The American Right has put forth a wide variety of defenses for laissez-faire, including: (1) a Calvinist work ethic that promised material success for a predestined elite; (2) Social Darwinism ("the survival of the fittest") of the William Graham Sumner variety; (3) strict construction of the Constitution, personified by Elihu Root; (4) a selfishness "ethic" based upon some form of Objectivism, à la Nathaniel Branden; (5) a belief that the free market delivers more goods for more people than any other system, à la Henry Hazlitt; (6) a conviction that capitalism is the economic system most in line with the Great Tradition of Western civilization, as Frank Meyer maintained; (7) a fear of being led down the "road to serfdom" (Friedrich Hayek); and (8) a moral affection for the humaneness of the free market (Wilhelm Roepke).

The list of alternative apologies for the free market could perhaps be extended. But for our present purposes this is enough. The question at hand is: Can the American right wing hope to make sense philosophically while calling upon such a hodge-podge of contradictory theories? It is readily apparent that *some* of the eight positions outlined above are diametrically opposed to one another. They differ sharply on such monumental topics as God, human nature, the legitimacy and purpose of the state, the nature of community, and so on. How can the American Right field a winning team when the players disagree about the objectives of the game?

Clearly, what conservatives need to do is to sit down and seriously ask themselves: What is the philosophy of American conservatism on the welfare state? On the one hand, the adherents of positions 5–8 could quite conceivably come to terms with the economic activism of the post–New Deal era. For the 1–4 contingent, on the other hand, the outlook for such a compromise is obviously very bleak. Indeed, it seems safe to say that in certain circumstances—for example, to help those who are destitute of food, clothing, shelter, and medical care—the proponents of positions 5–8 could actually favor government intervention, whereas the 1–4 team clearly could not. (The 3ers could perhaps amend the Constitution if they so desired.) Now, my intention here is not to argue the relative merits of the 5–8ers as opposed to those of the 1–4ers, but merely to show that the distance from the serene confines of political theory to the stormy battlefields of activism is not as great as it may at first seem.

The prospects for conservative advances on the practical level depend upon a clarification of the philosophical underpinnings of the Right. To continue with the example of welfare statism: if, on the one hand, conservatives should opt in theory for some form of positions 1–4, they must rush back to the works of Albert Jay Nock and Frank Chodorov and to the images of McKinley-Hoover Republicanism, perhaps polished up a bit with the new libertarian rhetoric, in order to present a coherent package of beliefs to the public. If, alternatively, conservatism should be defined along the lines of the 5–8ers, rightists can begin to contemplate recasting themselves as traditionalist friends of the common man and the little guy, with moral and patriotic orientations. We see, therefore, that a reliable understanding of the meaning of conservatism is a prior requirement for any attempt to revitalize the American Right.

The "pro-activism–anti-theory" group, moreover, has no objective yardstick for measuring victories or defeats. To cite a typical example, let us contrast how mainstream conservatives reacted to the Russian invasions of Hungary in 1956 and Czechoslovakia in 1969. In 1956 the American Right screamed its indignation against the liberals for their indecision, saying in effect, "Liberals! You have committed a terrible crime by not sending American military aid to the heroic Hungarian freedom fighters! Your heinous deed will never be forgotten." In 1969 the Right merely intoned knowingly, "Liberals . . . See, we told you so. Look at Prague. Those Communists aren't as decent as you thought they were." There is quite a theoretical gulf separating these two reactions. Now, if fifties conservatism had built its anticoexistence rhetoric on the firm philosophic grounds then offered by Frederick Wilhelmsen, L. Brent Bozell, or even Peter Viereck, it is highly unlikely that the Right would have interpreted the invasion of Prague any differently than it did the "rape of Budapest." In fact, however, the liberation rhetoric of many of the early conservatives was to a very great extent based upon a skin-deep neo-Wilsonian "philosophy" of crusading for the spread of democracy, or else upon pure machismo-jingoism of the sort made popular by Teddy Roosevelt. It was not very difficult for these conservatives to abandon a philosophy that merely amounted to fanciful stick waving.

Despite their almost complete abandonment of tough anti-Communism of any variety, whether it be metaphysical, Wilsonian, or imperialistic, mainstream conservatives appear totally unaware that they have surrendered one of the first principles of the movement. This is due to the fact that the American Right only vaguely sees itself as embodying a *system* of thought. Conservatives stroll calmly from rout to rout in the public arena, while unbeknown to them their entire theoretical structure is falling to pieces. Since the

44

conservative team has no clear game plan, it cannot weigh the results of the contest.

Another weakness from which a purely activist conservative stance suffers is that it is helpless to break out of media-imposed stereotypes. The media have decided which public figures should be labeled conservative. This has resulted in the current stagnation of conservative images—"vibes" in the vernacular—conveyed by the leading rightist personalities. For example, the media have chosen to label Senator Jesse Helms and Governor Reagan as conservative, while pompously describing Congressmen John Rousselot and Larry McDonald as "ultraconservative." It seems that those who dictate the terms of American politics are more than ready to call men conservatives if they can feel assured that by so doing they will reinforce the public impression of rightists as penny-pinching fat cats. All this leaves conservatives precious little to go on. As *National Review* has candidly observed, the Reagan-Buckley brand of conservatism appears to be "electorally vulnerable."

Why does the American conservative movement meekly go along with this thinning of its ranks by the media? When will conservatives realize that a whole range of diverse public symbols are in fact theirs? Among such symbols would be the big-city mayor of the old school: traditionalist, anti-Communist, strong on law and order, religiously oriented—a Richard Daley or Frank Rizzo. Or how about union leaders like AFL-CIO president George Meany? The antiabortion candidacy of Ellen McCormack in the 1976 Democratic primaries was surely a rightist symbol. And there are a host of others. Unfortunately, and surprisingly, the American Right tends to allow the leftist-dominated media to designate who are to be the true champions of conservatism. If the Right had a sound grasp of its basic philosophy, a situation like this could not arise. Conservatives could measure these different symbols of conservatism against the first principles of the movement.

In any event, rightists have gotten themselves into all kinds of difficulties by trying to advance the cause while carrying it, as Willmoore Kendall remarked, in their hips instead of their heads. But, as we noted before, a number of thinkers have *attempted* to define conservatism in postwar America, and although such activities have slowed down in recent years, it is to these definers that we must turn to begin our search for the real meaning of conservatism.

It seems fitting at this point, before plunging ahead to the various definitions of conservatism, to define what we mean by a definition of conservatism. There is an unmistakable "gut level" unity among rightists the world over. Through the years, for example, the names Franco, Rhee, Salazar, Batista, Chiang Kai-shek, and so on tended to evoke the sympathy of American conservatives. The pages of *National Review* and *Human Events* have periodically offered apologetic pieces describing the merits and answering the critics of the rightist governments of Chile, Rhodesia, South Africa, Spain, Brazil, Taiwan, and, until recently, Greece. In addition, American conservatives who engage in historical studies invariably express their admiration for the monarchial defenders of the old order against the revolutionaries in the 1789–1848 period, for the Mannheim-Kolchak "whites" in the 1918–1922 period, for the Nationalists against the "Loyalists" in civil-war Spain, etc. Surprisingly, this affinity between American and foreign conservatives is to be found even among the "remnant" rightists of the John Birch Society, who generally erect a mythical halo of saintliness and infallibility around the American Founding Fathers. For instance, the JBS once offered a series of reprints of conservative books called the Americanist Classics, which it said proclaimed the "ideals represented by America at its best"—ideals upheld by, among others, "the Korean Synghman Rhee." Now, any similarities between Patrick Henry, Samuel Adams, or even James Madison and John Adams, and Synghman Rhee, are not readily apparent. Yet these feelings of unity undeniably exist. It would seem that there is some sort of link between the various national manifestations of the right wing. When we speak of defining conservatism, we have in mind the fact that conservatives feel some sort of doctrinal kinship with their predecessors from earlier periods of history and with their comrades throughout the contemporary world.

It could perhaps be argued that any gut-level affections that may exist between, say, Habsburg restorationists and the Americans for Constitutional Action, or between Action Française and the Liberty Amendment Committee, are merely fictitious, an illusion spawned by a superficial system of political labels that equates one right wing with another. I contend, though, that despite the obvious disagreements between rightists on many practical matters, there does seem to be some substance to the conservative feelings of unity. Rightists *do* seem to demonstrate the same kinds of loyalties, dislikes, and even moods and temperaments in different countries and times. They invariably stress the importance of God, family, community, loyalty, and an awareness of man's imperfections, among other things. So, however far the philosophy of Integralisimo Lusitano may be from that of the English Distributists, or that of the Carlists from that of the White Citizens' Councils, it appears that at some root level conservatives are united. Let us now move on to discover the nature and unearth the source of these roots.

I have divided rightist thinkers into three categories. The first is composed of those whom I call "provincialist" conservatives, for they equate the essence of conservatism with the political traditions of a given country, generally their own. "Universalists" is the label I apply to conservatives whose philosophy transcends national and historical borders. Universalists fall into three different subcategories, treated below. Finally I turn to an individual whom I refer to as a "realist" conservative because his philosophy seems to encompass the other groups and to go a bit beyond them.

The Provincialist Conservative

The provincialist or sectarian conservative takes the political theories of his own national tradition to be the only legitimate form of rightist expression. This tendency is generally to be found among conservatives who devote most of their energies to the nitty-gritty of day-to-day political struggles. It therefore comes as no surprise that one of the prime exponents of rightism as quintessentially American is an individual who spends the bulk of his time fighting the good fight for the movement out on the public battlefield, namely M. Stanton Evans, columnist, lecturer, and former chairman of the American Conservative Union. Although Evans as a rule confines himself to waging conservative wars in the rough-and-tumble world of syndicated columns, radio broadcasts, political campaigns, and the like, he has on occasion ventured into the realm of theoretical inquiry, which is usually left to the armchair philosophers of the ivory tower. When functioning in his role as polemicist and activist of the Right, Evans does more for the conservative movement in one week than the vast majority of rightists will manage to do in an entire lifetime. It is for this very reason that one hesitates before commenting on one of his infrequent forays out of his natural habitat in the pages of *Human Events* and *Battle Line* into the thicket of *Modern Age*, an essentially intellectual and scholarly journal. After duly recording all his dedicated service to the conservative cause, however, I think it must be pointed out that Evans has also inflicted a certain amount of harm on the movement by seeming to believe that rightism in its truest sense is the sole possession of Anglo-Saxon pluralists who stand up for free enterprise.

In his widely publicized essay, "A Conservative Case for Freedom,"[6] which originally appeared in the Spring 1961 issue of *Modern Age* and was subsequently included in Frank Meyer's anthology of conservative thought, *What Is Conservatism?*, Evans attempts to exorcise from the conservative ranks just about every rightist who does not toe a delicate line between what he terms "libertarianism" and "authoritarianism." As for the "libertarians," we are told that they are wrong because "to exist in community . . . some kind of general equilibrium has to prevail." The "authoritarians" are equally in error because "virtue cannot be legislated."[7] By defining conservatism as the attempt "to insure that enough governmental authority exists to suppress criminal outcroppings of human weakness, but at the same time to insure that no man, or group of men, is vested with too much political power," Evans is obviously groping for some way to proclaim that American constitutionalism is the *only* authentic form of conservative government. Evans admits that putting his brand of conservatism into practice has "proved throughout the centuries to be a troublesome undertaking." Actually, he informs us, there has really been only one successful solution to the "dilemma of free government":

> . . . the problem . . . achieved its highest resolution in the compact on which the United States was based . . .
> In a word, the model answer to the dilemma of free government is the American constitution, founded in the counterpoise of interests of colonial North America and fused in the sagacious, powerful and combining mind of James Madison.[8]

In passages such as these it becomes clear that Evans' conservatism is something that the European Right could not live with, that the political systems of the Catholic Middle Ages could not be reconciled with, and that, indeed, the great classical Greco-Roman political philosophers could not be allied with. For our present purposes it is unnecessary to challenge Evans' belief in the uniqueness of the American system of government. We need only note that his definition of conservatism is, in reality, no definition at all. It is rather an attempt to demonstrate the inherent superiority of one form of government over all others. Evans leaves us no clue to the real meaning of the word conservatism as it is usually understood and as we hope to understand it in the present context, that is, as a philosophy that has been advanced by classical thinkers, by medieval theologians, and by rightist philosophers throughout the past two and a half centuries.

It should perhaps be noted in passing that Evans does admit the "fallibility" of the Constitution; throughout American history it "has, of course, achieved less than perfection." So he seems to be something less than a simon-pure ideologue. But any doctrine that urges us to idealize the political tradition of one nation above all others (not because it is *ours,* which could make sense, but because it is the best and truest tradition around), must be regarded as a falsification of conservatism. Whatever else may be said of it, the rightist tradition did not begin in 1776 or 1787, as Evans at times seems to be saying. In fact, Evans goes so far as to say that "traditional Western belief" has given us as its "secular by-products" the institutions of limited government and the market economy.[9] Now, even a cursory reading of Western history shows that traditional Western belief, in its Hebraic, Greek, Roman, or Christian representations, has only infrequently defended limited government and the market economy. Evans' thought is fatally handicapped by his idealistic picture of American constitutionalism.

The rightist patriot faces a perpetual temptation to proceed as Evans has done. To the reflective conservative, though, the urge to equate the Great Tradition of the West with its assorted temporary manifestations must be resisted at all costs. This does *not* mean that rightists cannot be patriots. In fact, quite the reverse is true. Conservatism, no matter how one defines it, has invariably been associated with the deep-seated human emotions of loyalty and reverence for family, locality, region, nation, etc. However, love for one's country does not imply a philosophical commitment to the proposition that the citizenry or the political presumptions of the nation are inherently superior to those of other lands. Consider the analogy of familial loyalty and love. We do not feel a kinship with our parents, brothers, sisters, children, and so on because we believe they are necessarily superior to members of other families. Similarly, patriotism is a virtue independent of the actions or be-

49

liefs of one's homeland. "My country right or wrong," G. K. Chesterton said, "is like 'My father sober or drunk.' We would like to have him sober but he remains our father even when drunk." The feelings of love, loyalty, and pride that swell up in one's chest when he hears "God Bless America" or "America the Beautiful" being played, or when he watches the flag go by in a dress parade at West Point, are not diminished in the least by one's qualms about, say, the wisdom of the First Amendment.

In reality, there is much to be bemoaned as well as much to be admired in the American system of government. The combination of liberty and authority that the Founding Fathers put together is not the only way of uniting the two. Unless conservatives wish to operate in a total historical and theoretical vacuum, they simply cannot find the "true" philosophy of the Right embodied in just *one* constitutional system—the American or any other. Besides being theoretically erroneous, such a stance would do a grave injustice to all the innumerable philosophers, politicians, and saints throughout the centuries who, despite their loyalty to the central themes of Western civilization, would look upon the secular democracy of twentieth-century America with a great deal of skepticism.

(Parenthetically, it is only fair to observe that one gets the feeling on reading Evans' other works that he is not quite the Wilsonian true believer in Americanism that his essay on freedom seems to indicate. He too feels the gut affinity with rightists the world over that most American conservatives do. His stands on abortion, internal security, and a host of other matters create a far tougher impression than his theories would appear to justify. This tendency to adore American institutions in a quasimystical manner while harboring basic rightist beliefs, likes, and dislikes that on a theoretical level would be hard to reconcile with rugged-individualist–libertarian rhetoric is also evident in the zestful and insightful conservative writing of his father, Medford Evans. Here we are apparently dealing with what the Bible refers to as "love damaging the root." Out of a deep and sincere love for American conservatism, especially as it has been expressed during the post–Civil War stage of its development, the Evanses and others like them tend to gloss over the real root assumptions of the Right. Thus, one can probably rest assured that had M. Stanton Evans lived fifty years ago in France, he would have chaired the Camelots du Roi with the same fervor with which he recently led the American Conservative Union.)

50

The late Frank S. Meyer was another American conservative who seemed to feel that rightism is the sole possession of constitutional republicans. Meyer hoped to reconcile the differences between the libertarian and traditionalist elements of the American right wing through a philosophy that came to be known as "fusionism." On the level of theory, fusionism claimed that individualism was the necessary basis for any society that wished to provide the possibility of a virtuous life. Fusionism offered a workable common ground for some of the factions of the American conservative coalition, and by so doing it helped to unify the Right during the early postwar years. It is safe to say that all conservatives, with the exception of the most doctrinaire libertarians and traditionalists, are extremely thankful to the sage of Woodstock for his service to the movement. He did much to keep it viable during some difficult years of its existence.

But Meyer was not content to leave things on a merely pragmatic level. To the contrary. In his eyes fusionism was not merely a practical approach, or one of the many legitimate manifestations of conservatism (which it definitely is), but *the only true expression of rightism.* As Meyer himself expressed it, fusionism is the only philosophy that is capable of overcoming "the nineteenth-century bifurcation of the Western tradition."[10] Like Evans, Meyer believed that the only system of government that has succeeded in reconciling "the tensed poles of Western thought . . . as never before or since" was the constitutional government of the United States of America:

> The division . . . of European thought between the emphasis upon virtue and valor and order and the emphasis on freedom and the integrity of the individual person was overcome [by] the men who created the Republic, who framed the Constitution and produced that monument of political wisdom, *The Federalist Papers . . .*[11]

> The men who settled these shores . . . established a constitution that for the first time in human history was constructed to guarantee the sanctity of the person and his freedom.[12]*

*Meyer frequently made reference in his writings to this "sanctity" of the individual's freedom. Indeed, his entire doctrine of conservative individualism rests in the end on metaphysical assumptions about the importance of freedom. This belief, in various garbs, has profoundly influenced

There is a contradiction in Meyer's thought, apparent upon close examination, that sheds a great deal of light on his fusionist philosophy. At times Meyer tells us that fusionism emerges by combining the theories of two distinct schools of thought. The process involves a "hard-fought dialectic" in which "differences of emphasis between libertarian and traditionalist cannot be avoided and should not be regretted. Conservatism has no monolithic party line." Again, more explicitly he writes, "Libertarian and traditionalist, as they deepen their understanding in a commonly based dialogue, can maintain a common front and a common struggle." On the other hand, Meyer could with great ease switch to a quite different line and maintain that the Great Tradition of the West is, in fact, fusionist! Hence he speaks often of how the tradition split *only* during the last century. In this role, while insisting that fusionism is somehow rooted in the conservatism of antiquity, Meyer frequently laments the "nineteenth-century struggle between classical liberalism and a conservatism that was too often authoritarian."[13] At such times Meyer seems to be asserting that the political theories of, say, the Manchesterians and the Bourbon emigrés had at one point been united. Of course, we must constantly keep in mind that Meyer, even when he professes to admire the Great Tradition before it "bifurcated," is convinced that "Western political theory on the European continent . . . never rose

---

the American Right. It would therefore seem worthwhile to consider this teaching of Meyer's in the light of orthodox religious principles.

Catholics, Protestants, and Jews differ on the precise nature of man's obligation to God. They agree, however, on one point: that the prime reason for man's existence on earth is to glorify God and do His will. Faith, sacraments, good works, *mitzvot* are the means to an end. Thus, it is absurd to speak of freedom as the foremost of all the transcendental values. At best, freedom presents the individual with an opportunity to pursue transcendental goals. It is not a transcendental goal or value by itself.

The state, the locality, the school, the family, and the individual are all sources of authority, which is ultimately derived from and subordinate to God. Each of these subdivisions of society has an area in which it contributes to the overall communal virtue. These areas should not be confused with one another. In a traditional society, for example, property belonged to individuals, children were under the authority of their parents, and the state sought to prevent severe outbursts of heresy and sin. Freedom, then, is not a positive value with religious significance, but a negative check that prevents the entities in the social structure from invading each other's spheres of authority and upsetting the natural and organic functions of community.

to the creation of a truly Western political philosophy of freedom."[14]

This is the third strain of fusionism that Meyer advances. In this stance he is quite content to divorce himself from traditional Western thought in no uncertain terms. He writes that "whether European intellectual history blesses us or not" is of no importance for fusionists. Brushing aside the criticism that "what is not in the tradition of Burke—or of the medieval synthesis—or of Plato—cannot call itself conservatism," he announces that the American system is the only "comparatively close approximation to the ideal" of a free and virtuous society.[15] When writing in this vein Meyer willingly severs his philosophy from its supposed roots in Judeo-Christian and classical Greek thought. As for the early Hebraic experiences under the judges, kings, and prophets, Meyer laments that "a social structure distorted the individual experience of transcendence," and the "potentialities for full individuation" that the Sinai experience had offered were "collectivized." The Greeks also blew their chance, according to Meyer, because "the Hellenic spirit was bound still by the necessity of expressing itself through a collectivity." This flaw "was an omnipresent limit upon [the] genius" of Greek classical thought and was "never overcome." Christendom similarly failed, in Meyer's view. The promising "possibilities" inherent in the doctrine of the Incarnation "have not been realized" because "the human heritage of the cosmological civilizations" has "distort[ed] its understanding." Indeed, this heritage of community succeeded in "stifling and destroying the development of the Western genius . . . in the political sphere." Happily, Meyer concludes that the three failures of the Western political genius to realize itself were not final and "the stage was set . . . and the United States was constituted," bringing the frustrating experience of twenty centuries to a satisfactory (and historical) conclusion.[16]

Three Frank Meyers thus emerge: the pragmatist, calling libertarians and traditionalists to a temporary coalition against their common enemies; the classicist, seeking reassertion of the Western tradition as it existed prior to the "bifurcation" of the nineteenth century; and the radical, rejecting the experience of the West in favor of the one true system of American fusionism. Meyer the pragmatist, as we noted before, was invaluable to the American Right; Meyer the classicist may, without too much presumption, be dismissed as a wishful thinker; while Meyer the radical, condemning the Hebrews, Greeks, and medieval Christians for their failure to anticipate James Madison's theories of government, is as good an example as any of a conservative provincialist.

Meyer's philosophy is perhaps better understood when we realize that underlying his thinking was the need to provide the post–World War II conservative movement with a working theoretical substratum. Meyer was forced to articulate a philosophy that could lend to the Blaine-McKinley-Hoover Republicanism of the 1868–1932 period some sort of continuity with classical philosophy and Judeo-Christian metaphysics. It was out of this yearning that fusionism was born.

At times the urge to portray one's own national traditions as the only possible means of incarnating conservatism becomes uncontrollable in Meyer's thought. For example, he often wrote that if virtue "is coerced by human force, it is meaningless." (Of course, the difficulty with statements of this sort is that there are so many degrees, forms, and institutions of coercion. Does coercion mean the threat of death? Imprisonment? Exile? Fine? Ostracism? Does it include force imposed by local governments? Communal groupings? Religious orders? Friends? Families? If, as Meyer always seems to be saying, a virtuous act is only one that is performed in a total vacuum of outside force, can *any* good deed be called "virtuous"?) Now, when one recalls that Meyer was unhappy with the ancient Hebrew monarchy, the Greek *polis,* the Catholic Middle Ages, the European Right, and even traditionalist-leaning American "New Conservatives" because all of them advocated some form of "forced virtue," the deficiencies of radical conservative provincialism become strikingly evident. Did Meyer seriously feel that all virtue prior to 1776 was "meaningless"? Were the innumerable saints and righteous men of two thousand years of Western history practicing a form of "meaningless" virtue because they lived in societies that sanctioned various kinds of institutional and familial coercion?

Willmoore Kendall once described Meyer as a "doctrinaire," and that would seem to be an apt description of the conservative provincialist. (One wonders how American provincialist conservatives would respond to a Spanish or Russian rightist who claimed that Integrism or the doctrine of the Third Rome represented "the highest resolution of the dilemma of just government"!) For the rightist in the post-1789 revolutionary era, the provincialist itch can lead to an almost ideological distortion of conservatism. By the term ideol-

54

ogy I refer, of course, to the neognostic utopian thinking that typifies much of the contemporary Left and holds that readjustment of man's outward institutions can bring about a significant change in human nature. The Communist, who is a prime example of the ideologue, believes that by altering man's economic system one can completely remake humanity and usher in paradise on earth. Similarly, other utopians throughout history, such as Saint-Simon, Auguste Comte, and Teilhard de Chardin (to cite just a few random examples from recent centuries), have offered other means of changing the given nature of humanity as it has always been known. It would be too much to put the rightist provincialist on a par with the leftist ideologue. Yet there are many similarities between a leftist who believes in "one true system" capable of satisfying all of mankind's needs and a rightist who feels that the ultimate fulfillment of Western civilization was the Philadelphia convention and who further claims that only under such a government can man's actions be deemed virtuous or moral.[17]

Professor Eric Voegelin, who has contributed so much to conservative thought with his scholarly dissection of ideological movements, has uncovered traces of rightist utopianism in such surprising places as the writings of Joseph de Maistre[18] and the Holy Alliance document of September 26, 1815 published in the names of the Austrian, Prussian, and Russian monarchies.*

In his recently published work *From Enlightenment to Revolution,* Voegelin describes de Maistre's tendency in many of his works but especially in *The Pope* to believe that a united Europe under papal supremacy could wipe out all the revolutionary and rationalist evils that were then beginning to shake the foundations of the West. Voegelin writes:

> That the critical situation of a whole civilization, which had been in the making for centuries, cannot be transformed into harmonious order overnight by an act of insight or by an agreement between intelligent people, or that something might be profoundly wrong not only outside Catholicism but

*The utopianism of the Holy Alliance, Voegelin says, is evident in its chiliastic, eschatological rhetoric. For that reason it is not quite comparable to the provincialist-conservative type of utopianism that we are now examining. Joseph de Maistre, though, is an excellent example of a normative provincialist conservative thinker.

within the Church itself, was not sufficiently clear to him . . .
In de Maistre as in Comte we sense the touch of enlightened
reason that blinds the working of the spirit.[19]

In the late 1960s, when the forces of rebellion were vigorously at
work to destroy the basic structures of American government, education, and law enforcement, Frank Meyer reacted to the problem
as de Maistre did in the eighteenth century. At a time when conservative intellectuals ranging from empiricists like James Burnham[20] and Donald Atwell Zoll[21] to the Catholic traditionalists of
Triumph were seriously questioning whether the American constitutional system was capable, in its present form, of defending itself,* Meyer was blissfully free of such qualms. To him the system
would solve all problems. It was inconceivable to him that anyone
could question "the traditions of the Constitution and the Founding
Fathers."[22] He refused to question the system; it was "the ordering
principle, fount and end of social being."[23] Meyer's response was
an almost exact replica of de Maistre's call for papal order, except
that Meyer substituted constitutionalism for Catholicism. As
Thomas Molnar pointed out at the time:

> All Meyer does is to state that such restoration of order is
> possible *if* the Constitution and the laws are enforced. But the
> whole debate hinges on the question why are they not en-
> forced? . . . As Meyer's example shows, it is easier to engage
> in the magic repetition of pleasing words than to analyze,
> without illusions, a situation.[24]

Molnar's criticism of Meyer closely parallels Voegelin's of de
Maistre. The rightist provincialist seems unable, because of his
total commitment to a given set of conservative symbols (those of
his own nation or religious faith, for example), to uncover the
sources of deep social problems or to advocate *original, yet conservative* solutions to such ills. Meyer, like de Maistre before him,
made the two interrelated mistakes of provincialist conservatism.
Both men mistook a certain set of conservative symbols for conservatism proper. Meyer went so far as to write that conservatism
is not "some collection of . . . attitudes" but merely "a devotion to
the restoration of our tradition."[25] Second, both men were determined to defend the symbols of rightism to the bitter end, even if

---

*The empiricists lamented the lack of a means to survive, while the
traditionalists, digging a bit deeper, found that a reason and therefore a
will to survive was missing.

the essentials should perish in the process. The same sort of thinking is evident in the position of various European restorationists who declined, during the twenties and thirties, to support the rightist governments of Dollfuss, Horthy, Franco, Salazar, and Pilsudski because they were not "legitimate." Here again, the general good—a conservative government—must be sacrificed to maintain one's pure devotion to the specific form that rightism took during the Middle Ages. This line of reasoning, whether it comes from a die-hard Bourbon restorationist opposing post-1883 monarchist efforts because he rejects the claims of the dukes of Orléans, or from Frank Meyer advocating "freedom of the person" in the face of anarchy and insurrection,* is provincialist conservatism at its self-crippling, ideological worst.

Let it be said, however, despite all the foregoing, that Frank Meyer was a dedicated conservative who contributed much to the good fight for the Right in America, just as M. Stanton Evans is doing today. But conservatives cannot let their respect for and gratitude to these men for their many accomplishments blur the fact that both failed to define conservatism so as to do justice to the history of the movement and to its relevance in diverse cultural, national, and religious contexts.

There are several other schools of conservative thought that manage to overcome the provincialist's urge to idealize a particular system. These express their rightism in terms that are applicable in different times and places. Accordingly, I have labeled the three thinkers outlined below "universalist" conservatives; their philosophies meet the qualifications of our "definition of a definition of conservatism." They will henceforth command a great deal of our interest.

The Metaphysical Conservative

Professor Frederick D. Wilhelmsen of the University of Dallas, a former editor of *Triumph*, is one of the most prolific and articulate

---

*Of course, the rebellion of the sixties did eventually quiet down, but no thanks to the Right. Had the situation continued, or worsened, it would have been interesting to see how great a destruction of the "permanent things" Meyer would have tolerated in his desire to maintain the fusionist position. Would he have admitted at some point that a "free" and "open" society is incapable of curing *some* problems?

metaphysical conservatives[26] on the American scene. An exceptionally broad thinker, Wilhelmsen easily transcends the misguided patriotism that has caused so many American rightists to be taken in by the provincialist-conservative fallacy. He has, in fact, loudly lamented the "scandal of ignorance in the American academic community about just what the European Right is and means." American conservatism as a whole is also guilty in this respect, having "shown itself alarmingly naive in what often seems to be a principled rejection of any serious consideration of things politically conservative that takes place outside the Anglo-Saxon diaspora of Western conservatism. . . ."[27] Rewardingly, for our present purposes, Wilhelmsen's own theories are largely free of such naiveté.

Briefly stated, the basis of Wilhelmsen's conservatism is religion, or more specifically, the Catholic faith. (He has written that Protestantism is incompatible with what he calls "incarnational politics" and Judaism is not so much as mentioned in his works.) The Christian religion, he says, is "marked by an internal experience which consists of two moments," the first being acceptance of and dependence on God, while the second is

> our response to the call to sanctify the whole of creation . . . This means . . . that whereas there are only seven sacraments there are as many potential sacramentals . . . as there are beings themselves. The sacramentalization of the real, be it the high act of anointing kings in medieval Christendom or the picturesque blessing of the Portuguese fishing fleet today, is the essence of what I would like to call the *civilizing* aspect of the Incarnation. We are called upon not only to save our souls but, in so doing, to save the world.[28]

This process of "hallowing the world," as he calls it, is the only true purpose of human endeavor, according to Wilhelmsen. Ideally speaking, our attempt to "sanctify the real" should pervade all spheres of human activity. Thus Wilhelmsen tells us that "sacramentalizing the real includes the political and social orders." The ultimate goal of public affairs, for a Catholic, is to bring about the establishment of a "truly Christian Order of Things," whose "customs have been minted in the sacral—whose corporate existence is thus a sacramental and an actual grace gestured to the world . . ."[29]

Wilhelmsen sees metaphysical politics as tending to "weave a golden web of sacrality around the world" by two means: one conscious, the other organic. By conscious effort he refers to the ongoing attempt by Christians to effect "an extension of the sacramental system by which Christ saves through His Church." The organic processes of a theocentric society would, further, automatically result in "the yeast of faith ever working its health into the body politic."

Wilhelmsen avoids the pitfall of equating metaphysical political beliefs with the substance of faith itself. He strongly emphasizes that the former are merely the natural derivative of the latter. "Incarnational politics . . . add a dimension to the political order. Politics remain politics; [they are] not transformed into religion."[30] Faith, being transcendent, is invisible in this world except to the extent that man articulates it, either through religion proper or through its various symbolizations and incarnations. Thus:

> The sacredness of the person and the eternal relationship he bears to God through Christ are truths of an order which is not human, but these truths act within the bowels of society as Divine Seeds, conceiving in time a temporal order both personal and free. This order is Christendom. It is not the City of God, but it is within that City, and it is what it is because it is the child of Faith.[31]

Wilhelmsen is idealistic; one might even be tempted to call him lyrical or romantic. He harbors high hopes for the potentialities inherent in the human situation. As a result of this, he has even attempted to tone down somewhat the natural rightist rejection of utopian blueprints for society. "Models" for the perfect society are necessary, in his view, not as practical goals to be realized in the here and now (as the true totalitarian utopian would believe), but to lift the human mind "above the pragmatically given." In fact, Wilhelmsen goes a step further and believes that social and political models are indispensable at this troubled juncture in history, for

> if man, Western man, cannot raise his heart beyond the miserably mediocre moment in which he lives, if he cannot at least see "the distant hills," he will risk nothing and he will gain nothing. He will lack the charismatic fire needed to purge his own miserably corrupt civilization, not only of injustice and materialism, but even of gnostic utopianism itself.[32]

Despite his penchant for expressing his ideas in a flowing poetic style, and despite his belief in the need for paradigmatic standards and goals for society, Wilhelmsen is not a wishful thinker constructing theoretical castles out of thin air. He believes that his vision (which in the early stages of his career he termed "the conservative vision") was, for all practical purposes, realized in the Catholic Europe of the Middle Ages. It was there that sacramental politics reached its fullest implementation. It was there that religious men, well aware that "the meaning of existence is fundamentally theological," established governments and cultures in which "everything in any sense claiming title to existence was given a religious significance." The success of the medieval endeavor was manifest in every sphere of social existence:

> Medieval man sacramentalized the whole of being. This sense of the symbolic issued into a fruitful and dense mingling of things formally distinct. Thus the Holy Roman Emperor wore a blue star-spangled robe, representing the arc of the heavens, and he carried the imperial globe representing the world. He symbolized the temporal fellowship of all Christians in Christendom and his coronation in Rome at the hands of the Pope signified the very dependence of the globe of the world on the creative will of God . . .
>
> As with political existence so with man's life in time and space . . . the local church building [was] the extension, the situation, of the Incarnation. The church building, in turn, stands in the same analogical relation to cemeteries, chapels and wayside crosses. In this manner the Church spreads through the open spaces and hallows the land.
>
> The symbolization of space is paralleled by that of time . . . The here-and-now takes on a sacred awesomeness psychologically compelling medieval man to make himself the center of the physical cosmos. The eyes of God are upon him . . . Hell is at his feet and heaven just above his head . . .
>
> I am convinced that this medieval dream of this unity of all things is the mythic foundation for what I would call the conservative vision . . .[33]

It is important to recognize that Wilhelmsen's theories of "incarnational" or "sacramental" politics are not merely an empirical assessment of man's nature and his yearning to embody that nature in symbolic form. There are many secular anthropologists, sociologists, and historians who could readily testify to this human propensity to seek transcendence in the mundane. Wilhelmsen, though, parts company with such thinkers over their rejection of the element of *essential truth*, which must be the starting point for any legitimate sacramentalization of politics in particular or society in general. Once, after a lengthy discussion of the question of the individual's right to dissent from the orthodoxy of his community, Wilhelmsen concluded that a society that is not based upon religious truth has no ultimate claim to silence dissidents. In the final analysis only truth may claim obedience:

> . . . where the public orthodoxy is guaranteed by transcendence, by the Word of God, then the truths of the soul and of society . . . are theoretically guaranteed. Beyond this guarantee, which can be had only as a gift and as a blessing, *there is no other for any human society born upon this earth.*[34] (Italics added.)

Truth, or more precisely, God-given truth, is the only reality upon which to launch political or social endeavors. According to Wilhelmsen, in fact, divine revelation is the only rational grounding for life itself. He has severely attacked Eric Voegelin for writing that the ultimate truth about the "question of the Ground of Being" (God) is that there is "no answer." To Wilhelmsen a position of this sort represents a complete refutation of life itself, because existence is conceivable only if it is to be considered real in some ultimate metaphysical sense. As he expressed it in a highly critical review of the fourth volume in Voegelin's *Order and History* series, *The Ecumenic Age:*

> What matters, for Voegelin, as the late Willmoore Kendall once put it to me, is not whether Moses ever lived or not; what matters is the "Mosaic experience" . . .
> . . . the entire question of the "historicity" of Christ and His Resurrection annoys Voegelin; he finds it vulgar . . . But, Dr. Voegelin, "if He be not risen"—in the words of St. Paul—then I for one don't give a damn about St. Paul's experience of Him . . . Dr. Voegelin is very cranky about the Resurrection but unless It happened his entire speculation about history is worthless; but then everything else is equally worthless.[35]

It is now possible for us to summarize Wilhelmsen's conservatism. The core of it is Catholicism, which he holds to be the one true faith. The Faith alone provides politics, philosophy, and life with rhyme and reason. A society that is dedicated to its faith is legitimate and will embody its beliefs in its institutions.

Is metaphysical conservatism possible only in a Catholic society? Wilhelmsen seems to think so. I would argue, however, that any community of men that acknowledges the governance of God will inevitably function in accordance with Wilhelmsen's theories. Even a nation composed of differing religious faiths can exhibit a form of metaphysical conservatism if its heritage provides a frame of reference for such an undertaking. (The American tradition does.) In a pluralist society, of course, metaphysical conservatism would stress those areas of religion and morality in which the citizenry is in general agreement.

The logical conclusion that issues from these theories is that conservatism as a public cause cannot succeed until the secular modern age has played itself out. Wilhelmsen has quite naturally reached just such a conclusion:

> . . . we conservatives cannot cure the modern world: we do not hold the power, nor is it likely to pass into our hands . . .[36]

> In a word every typically Catholic institution in the political and social order [has] either disappeared or [has been] reduced to a simulacrum of its ancient status . . .
> We Catholics have been robbed of our civilizing role in history. Living in a wholly secularist world, we have nothing to do in history.[37]

> The old European Christendom . . . its rich cultural diversity, its personal individualism and patchwork of small property, its shrines, its liberating chaos—these things can have no place in a world committed to the principle of technological and collectivist barbarism.[38]

The goal of sacramental politics in the current epoch, according to Wilhelmsen, is to wait for the modern world to finish "its last agony." The end is near, for "the age that began with the Renaissance is thrashing on a bed of death prepared by history."[39] Here, where he combines a pessimistic prognosis for the age of secularism with hope for the future, Wilhelmsen's originality as a metaphysical conservative becomes clear. Despite his personal affection for the pervasively religious medieval structure, he feels that it would be a mistake simply to identify "sane political life with the

62

ancien régime." To do so would be attractive but extremely dangerous for the cause of true metaphysical conservatism, for it would cause Christians to "abandon any effort . . . to . . . truly incarnate the Word of God in history." This error has paralyzed counterrevolutionary thought during the past two centuries. Wilhelmsen calls it the "Integrist temptation." "Integrists are restorationists," he writes. Though heroic, legitimist politics is also necessarily tragic. According to Wilhelmsen, the Integrist believes that

> [since] a sacral politics existed at such a time in history, the very same set of institutions that marked such a polity must be restored to its integrity . . . To a thoroughgoing Integrist the sacral *figures* he perceives as having marked an older political order must become the political *ground* of any new Christian order.[40]

Wilhelmsen is forced to admit sadly that "because he is so fascinated by his own tradition's historical models," the Integrist is doomed. He is unable to resurrect a set of symbols that his countrymen no longer find appealing:

> . . . the Integrist cannot react intelligently—imaginatively and creatively—to his own situation in time. He [sees] that the restoration is not about to come. Therefore he despairs . . .[41]

Although fearful that "Integrist temptations will paralyze our wills," Wilhelmsen believes it still possible at this late date to "seize the moment for the sake of Eternity."[42] He feels that once the world is "purged of the temptation to play God," it will inevitably be "waiting to be hallowed."[43] At that time the task of the metaphysical conservative will be enormous; the Faith will "arise out of the new catacombs and be faced with sanctifying a society that is neither humanist nor humane."[44]

Christians will have to develop new symbols, "figures," and "sacramentals" to give substance to the incarnational politics of the postmodern era. Wilhelmsen is convinced that, although the new symbols of sacramentalism will require much originality to formulate, the process will gradually become easier as the eternal truths of faith become more vibrant for postmodern man. "The need to fashion icons symbolic of the timeless is rooted in all mankind," he says.[45]

Wilhelmsen is exceptionally versatile. He has even begun to lay the groundwork for these new concretizations of metaphysical conservatism. Electronics, technology, mass-media communication, personality and familial cults, and neotribalism are frequently suggested in his writings as appropriate figures and means to incarnate the truths of eternity in the societies of the future. "Sanity in these matters," he cautions, "involves never confounding ground with figures."[46] The figures of sacramentalism may change, but for men or nations of faith they can always be "hallowed."

In the realm of politics Wilhelmsen is equally original and broad-minded. Personally he describes himself as a Spanish Carlist, which would seem to imply that he is some sort of doctrinaire agrarian-corporate monarchist. However, I think we must excuse him on this point, just as he has excused that brilliant Spanish conservative philosopher Donoso Cortes for his "preference for the traditional Catholic monarchy of the Middle Ages." Wilhelmsen cautions us that "political philosophers ought not to deny their fellow practitioners existential and historical preferences." But in truth, Wilhelmsen's conception of a just civil order is anchored, like his other theories, to something firmer than the rival claims of the Spanish succession. As he writes concerning Donoso Cortes:

> . . . behind Donoso's institutional predilections there lies a philosophy which transcends [them] as well because it purports to teach us something about Power itself, no matter where, or in what historical moment in time, or under whatever form it might exist, including—of course—under the form of democracy.[47]

Clearly, then, Wilhelmsen is not your run-of-the-mill Carlist. His admission that under certain cultural or historical circumstances even democracy can be reconciled with the essential features of conservative political theory indicates the clear distinction in his thinking between "form" and "ground." Few men of the Right have recognized this truth. By Wilhelmsen's reasoning, the predicament that the Royalists faced in nineteenth-century France in the person of liberal Bourbon kings or claimants, and that currently confronts Spanish rightists in the person of King Juan Carlos, is in reality no problem at all. To be sure, a rightist owes historical, sentimental, traditional, and mythical loyalty to the symbols through which conservatism is articulated in his own local context. Should these symbols prove self-defeating, however, or even simply no longer useful, conservatives must weigh carefully their priorities and conclude, in certain cases according to the dictates of prudence, that content must take precedence over form.

It is not important for our present purposes to illustrate exactly how both monarchy and democracy, agrarianism and technology, can be equally suitable forms for the embodiment of metaphysical conservatism. Let it be noted, though, that monarchy and agrarianism have a long history of rightist apologetics behind them. Democracy has also found many impressive apologists on the Right, most of them obviously operating within the Anglo-Saxon tradition. In fact, one of the major areas of rightist theory to which postwar American conservatives have applied themselves has been the attempt to work out some form of democratic pluralism that would not be at variance with the basically theocentric truths of Western civilization and its traditions. And technology? The traditional American capitalist Right, born in the Robber Baron age and resurrected in the fifties, has produced a sizable literature that has sought (whether it has succeeded is another matter) to imbue technology with a conservative essence. Wilhelmsen himself has done pioneering work with his efforts to arrive at a "sacramentalization of the new technology." In any event, the theoretical systems that seek to justify the various forms of rightist symbolization are unimportant at this moment. (They will assume monumental importance later on in this work.) The central themes of metaphysical conservatism have for our present purposes been arrived at.

In the first place, metaphysical conservatism is at war with the twin heresies of the Left: relativism, which preaches the inaccessibility of both God and truth, and ideology, which reduces the reality of human existence to fit certain fanciful theories and then seeks to remedy the situation by forcing changes in the makeup of humanity. The metaphysical conservative rejects relativism because its negation of all values and all truths contradicts religious faith, which lies at the root of his beliefs. Ideology, by denying that human nature is radically flawed and by demanding a magical change in the apparent facts of creation, also conflicts with the truths of traditional religion, which views human nature as essentially constant. Thus, metaphysical conservatism as a negative philosophy opposes any attempt to remove God from the world or to negate the legitimacy of His laws.

On the positive side metaphysical conservatism realizes that revealed truths, besides influencing man's life directly through transcendental rituals like the sacraments in the case of Catholicism, or the commandments in the case of Judaism, and besides prohibiting evil behavior, must permeate every fiber of man's communal existence to remain viable in the life of a society. Whether the form is monarchy, as it was for the Carlists; or corporatism, as it was for Salazar; or pluralist democracy, as it was for John Courtney Murray; or free enterprise, as it was for Wilhelm Roepke, is of no essential consequence. The key to the good and the just society is not the external forms that the government and communal existence happen to take. These forms must not, of course, clash with the social context in which they are advanced. The metaphysical conservative is not blind to the influences of religion, national characteristics, and traditions. He understands the important role they play. He would not attempt to offer John Hallowell's sacramentalized democracy* to the pious Navarrian Carlists, nor would he offer the Carlists' sacramentalized monarchy to the Dixiecrat agrarians of the Black Belt. However, he would insist that the root assumptions behind each and every form of goodly existence must be theological and subject to the transcendental norms that govern all men.

To the metaphysical conservative the center of the national body is the soul. If the soul is well, that is, if it submits itself to the kingship of God, then society will be healthy and this health will naturally permeate the institutions of communal and individual life, whether those institutions are technological or agrarian, democratic or monarchial. To the metaphysical conservative the success or failure of society is not measured by its GNP or nuclear first-strike capacity, but by its *spiritual* state. Consequently, he believes that the job of incarnating faith in the temporal realm is not primarily a political one. To cure a sick society—a society that denies God—one does not begin by winning elections but by reeducating the populace in accordance with the divine truths via the schools, the media, and other communal means.

In summation, *the metaphysical conservative rejects relativism and ideology on the basis of transcendental truths, which he seeks to translate into the temporal realm.*

*Hallowell is a conservative thinker who on the basis of a deep, in his words "mystical" Christianity has worked out a theoretical defense of democracy (*The Moral Foundations of Democracy*). Although he is uncomfortable with the conservative label, his theories are a unique contribution to traditionalist apologetics.

The Empirical Conservative

The rationalist or empirical conservative is the forgotten member of the right-wing team.* Historically speaking, though, skeptical rightism has a long and dignified tradition, numbering among its theoretical champions David Hume and Henry Adams, noted literary figures like Nathaniel Hawthorne and William Butler Yeats, and activists of whom Charles Maurras (during his public career) would be a notable example. Still, despite the impressive quality of its leading figures, naturalist rightism has never become a mass movement, least of all in America, where the conservative tradition has generally had some sort of religious orientation.

The starting point of empirical conservatism is its refusal to acknowledge the existence of divine truths. This immediately sets it apart from metaphysical conservatism. The empirical conservative's adherence to the theories of rightism is based upon a rational assessment of the realities of the human condition, that is, of man's needs and his limitations. There are few empirical conservatives of significant intellectual stature in America today. Professor Donald Atwell Zoll, author of numerous books and articles, is a notable exception.** Master of a style of writing that combines erudition and depth with zest and humor, he has carried the case for empirical conservatism to the public for almost twenty years. During this period he has launched salvos of friendly criticism against the American Right on any number of issues and has in his own words "gained a reputation as a Tory irregular and discovered . . . that he was not in the conservative mainstream." Zoll has offered cartloads of original suggestions to the American conservative movement (e.g., his advocacy in 1969 of "some new Locrian code" to fight the

*Although mainstream conservative journals often treat Objectivism and other libertarian isms as rightist, it should be fairly clear that the Rands, Brandens, Hospers, and others represent not merely a distorted branch of the movement, but the direct antithesis of everything the Right has stood for throughout history. They do not attempt to work out realistic political and social theories on the basis of empirical observation, but seek to build ultrarationalist, *a priori* utopian constructions. As a result, they cannot be classed with the empirical conservatives. Of course, libertarianism of a traditionalist and moral type, such as Jeffersonian agrarian or McKinley Republican libertarianism, is a different story.

**James Burnham, author of *Suicide of the West* and columnist for *National Review*, is another conservative of note who bases his rightism not upon religious considerations but upon solely empirical assessments.

New Left),[48] has denied the conservative credentials of leading American rightist politicians (i.e., Goldwater in 1964), and has cast as conservatives men commonly conceived of as liberals (e.g., Stevenson and Kennedy).[49]

Plainly, Zoll is not the typical American rightist. Upon further analysis, however, he emerges as not quite the nonconformist that first impressions would indicate. In fact, Zoll has arrived at positions that could generally be identified with those of the traditionalist Right. Naturally, his reasons for maintaining such beliefs are radically different from those of most of his colleagues. He has accepted the teachings of the Right not because they are true on a metaphysical or ultimate level, not because the human soul (as the term is used in a religious context) testifies to them, but because they are readily apparent to the student of history and human nature.

Empirical conservatives base their system upon a clear, unsentimental, and therefore nonutopian view of the human situation. As Zoll puts it:

> One of the strengths of historical conservatism has been its consistently acute evaluation of the limitations of human nature . . . Conservatism, with a kind of weary forbearance, has refused to be misled by the fragile optimisms and myopic meliorisms of the sentimentalized views of other broad political persuasions.[50]

The empirical conservative is a skeptic in the truest sense of the word. Because of his naturalist bent he denies God and revelation, but at the same time he refuses to believe the fanciful dogmas of utopians and revolutionaries and instead feels with George Santayana that in the long run "no specific hope about distant issues is likely to be realized." Jeffrey Hart aptly described the pessimism of the nonbelieving conservative when he wrote of David Hume:

> If Hume did not accept the Christian eschatology, he nevertheless based his politics upon its negative implications: salvation is not to be sought in the political realm and to do so would be disastrous. Hume's detachment from ultimate historical hope . . . suggests a thoroughly absorbed experience of the world, and an educated meditation on history; it requires, in the absence of religious hope, a severe discipline of the sensibility.[51]

Zoll has greatly broadened the traditional view of pessimistic empirical conservatism by drawing heavily upon recent scientific advances in the fields of analytical psychology, psychoanalysis, and neuropsychology. For example, Zoll believes that the analytical psychology of Carl Jung and Erich Neumann "offers an account of the human personality" that "squares more completely with conservative opinion then any other contemporary view." Jung's emphasis upon "the limits of the rational powers of the individual in relation to the psyche's irrational component" reaffirms one of the basic points of traditionalist conservatism, Zoll notes. Following analytical theory, Zoll believes that we are all governed by forces, loyalties, drives, and passions that, except in isolated individuals or at infrequent intervals, are never broken. Since these subconscious instincts predate the emergence of man's rational faculties, they are extremely powerful. Among them are the instincts that bind men in a suprarational allegiance to their families, localities, and nations; that prompt men to follow personality cults such as those surrounding saints, patriotic heroes, and in our "secular" age sports and show-business stars; that cause men to seek self-fulfillment not as isolated entities but as members of religious, national, local, familial, or fraternal groups.

In Jungian psychology these drives are associated with a *collective unconscious,* which is in Zoll's words "the source of consciousness itself and is the area of communication between the individual and the psychic force of the universe."[52] As far as the negative and distasteful components of the *collective unconscious* are concerned, Zoll feels that they can substitute for the older rightist doctrine that finite man is permanently flawed by original sin.

Zoll does not accept Jungianism lock, stock, and barrel. He usually qualifies his presentation of the Swiss psychologist's theories with phrases like "according to Jung," "Jung's account," etc. His naturalistic conservatism is not tied to just one of the physical sciences, but draws upon biological studies of "innate releasing mechanisms," neurological experiments with "trapped universals," and studies in cybernetics. From all of these disciplines Zoll has arrived at two broad conclusions:

> (1) Human nature contains crucial extraexperiential, transpersonal content, and psychic inheritance looms as a major factor in behavior; (2) Individual human behavior and culture rest on the existence of universals, present as innate structure

in the personality, as archetypal sign stimuli, both natural and supernormal and present as cultural artifact.[53]

Thus, empirical conservatism as understood by Zoll does not stop with a mere negation of the wild theories of various leftist utopians. It offers positive guidelines for ordering society that are in essential agreement with those of the traditionalist Right. Conservatives have always stressed the importance of community in human endeavor. Zoll agrees that "it is impossible to conceive of man separated from society." This is due to the existence of the collective unconscious, which influences man through "archetypes"; Zoll (following Jung) defines these as "collective images . . . arising contemporaneously with the primordial psyche which pre-dates human consciousness . . . act[ing] upon man as a cultural cohesion."[54]

This "cultural cohesion" impels man to articulate his innermost psychic drives through symbol and myth:

> According to Jung, psychic energy transfers are involved in the relationship between the collective and individual unconscious. Surpluses are produced and channeled into social inter-relationships, usually in symbolic form. In briefest terms, this is the causation of culture. Psychic energy transformed into symbol is observable through the mythopoetic realm.
> . . . this collective process is viewed through archetypal cores that reappear also in symbolic form. Jung calls these "motifs" and holds them to be universal, and from this implies the universality of human nature.[55]

The similarity of Zoll's teaching to that of normative metaphysical conservatives becomes even more evident when he goes on to say:

> . . . the analytical psychologists by giving attention to the non-cognitive elements in human personality have restored myth, symbol, poetry, religious expression and other like concerns to serious attention.[56]

Of course, Zoll does not ascribe transcendental truthfulness to "myth, symbol, poetry, religious expression," and so on, as do metaphysical conservatives. But he is in total accord with them on the vital importance these factors have in the existence of individuals as well as communities. In other words, the empirical conserva-

70

tive, having examined man in a purely naturalistic manner and having weighed the evidence of history, is keenly aware of the basic human need somehow to break out of a merely temporal, secular existence. He is invariably the ally of other conservatives who also support the social cohesives of family, community, religion, property, and the like, though for profoundly different reasons.

Translating his theories from the realm of the abstract to that of the practical, Zoll has offered a huge variety of proposals as to how conservatives can reshape society in a more rightist or realistic manner. For example, he has lamented the lack of conservative interest in "the problem of community." To Zoll, "historical conservatism has been especially sensitive to the conservancy of the community," and this has always been the Right's "elemental linkage with the anxieties and aspirations of the vast majority of men." Unfortunately, the postwar American conservative revival was crippled from the start by "indigenous American right-wing preferences for nineteenth-century individualism." This disability was, for Zoll, a tragedy of major proportions:

> Conservatism, the arch paladin of community, became—and surely in the public image it became—the champion not only of individualism, but also of those other post-nineteenth-century innovations that reshaped human living patterns, the most prominent of which was the natural exploitation, centralization, urbanization and *anomie* that the age introduced. The community was harassed by the thesis that human conditions of life ought to be predicated upon the ease of consumption in contrast to the primordial requirements of man.[57]

Zoll feels that conservatives must adhere to the traditional position of "encourag[ing] men to 'love their little platoon,' but in order for them to do so we must somehow keep the 'little platoon' a going concern."[58] This can be accomplished by a revival of what he terms the "civic ethic," which for all practical purposes is simply traditional communal morality. The result of this would be

> the renewal or recovery of social harmony, the encouragement of social friendship, the rule of tranquility and benevolence.
> . . . In sum, the object of conservatism is *social friendship*, the moderating of animosity by the tightening of the collective moral bonds, the depiction of a collective ethical purpose.[59]

Forever the empiricist, Zoll does not posit his ethical constructions as eternal values in a metaphysical sense. His "civic ethic" represents nothing more than

> the novel manifestations of instinctual universals and social accumulations [which] preserve . . . a contact with the most elemental and nondifferentiated strata of being. The ethical mandate is a summons to participate in the nature of nature.[60]

These moral rules, which "enforce, often stringently, both the latent instinctual demands of the individual psyche and the communal paradigms and objectives," are remarkably similar to the transcendental morality of orthodox faith. However, in accordance with his naturalism Zoll reassures us that the ethical imperative can be established by a "rudimentary mode of perception" that includes "the discovery of community, natural order, and the deontological features of that natural order."[61]

Zoll's grasp of the intricacies of empirical conservatism is matched by his ability to think along highly creative lines within the philosophical framework he has put forth. Like Wilhelmsen he has urged conservatives not to confuse "form" with "essence." It is rewarding to quote Zoll at some length here, for he strongly parallels Wilhelmsen on several important points:

> . . . contemporary conservatism is at a loss to know what to conserve . . . What it ought to be concerned about are *essences*, those natural paradigms that underlie human social institutions and practices. Such essences, derivable from the objective order of nature, are not identical to human conventions that may be equated with *forms*, transient configurations. Currently, the conservative defense of "tradition" tends to be the conservation of social forms instead of essences, but in placing its emphasis here, conservatism runs the risk of jeopardizing concern about and recognition of the imperative essences. Let us suppose the family to be a "natural" social institution . . . It would seem altogether reasonable to "conserve" the family institution [and] . . . to structure human practices in accord with this natural directive. But such a conservation seeks to preserve the essence of the institution; it can be quite flexible regarding the form. It need not seek to expressly conserve the form of family life typical, let us say, of the American middle classes in the nineteenth century, especially if such a formal conception of the family does not appear efficacious in a later era and if such a resolute insistence upon

the form of family organization impairs the continuity of the essential institution.[62]

Zoll has urged caution in presenting the distinction between form and essence to the conservative rank-and-file. He feels that for the vast majority of men forms tend to lose their vitality and ultimately their compelling character when divorced from essences. The average man is generally incapable of manning the conservative barricades in defense of a given form when he realizes that, in reality, the form is of no significance except as a symbolization of some archetypal essence or motif. As a practical matter, it is best to leave the forms of conservatism at any given moment in history somewhat hazily intertwined in the popular mind with the essential core that imbues them with their only actual relevance.

Zoll does believe, however, that certain institutional forms are better suited than others to the task of embodying the universal motifs. He maintains, for example, that monarchy is far superior to mass-suffrage democracy in fulfilling the hierarchal and communal needs of man. Yet he realizes that there are so many cultural variables involved in formulating political and social forms that it is extremely difficult to lay down hard-and-fast rules on how best to satisfy the demands of the collective unconscious in all realms and under different religious, cultural, and historical conditions.

According to Zoll, the question of changing forms should merely be of pragmatic interest to conservatives. Basically, he feels that changing a form is not harmful provided that the new form is still an adequate means of representing the archetypal essences. If the people at some point in history grow tired of the old forms and demand that they be reformed, it is the job of conservatives to perform, in Zoll's words, a "sleight of hand," which has been done "all throughout history," and make sure that the new forms remain true to the realities of the human condition. The natural means at the conservatives' disposal are public and private communication and education.

Should conservatives ever advocate or originate changes? Yes, answers Zoll; if they discern a new mood in the air, they should seize the opportunity and seek to translate these new feelings into terms that are consistent with human nature, empirically known. Furthermore, this process is inevitable, for mankind has in itself a certain "restlessness" that periodically opts for new forms. Conservatives should be aware of this and not venture to swim against

73

the tide except where the tide is decidedly wrong and incompatible with the demands of nature and the "civic ethic."

Deprived of the theistic orientation of other traditionalist conservatives, Zoll does not view the past two hundred years of world history as a period of decline, heading for some sort of apocalyptic conclusion. The metaphysical Right, he says, possesses "a sense of eschatological drama, a Dantesque imaginative fervor," and "a melancholy grandeur." Though held with "obvious intensity and sincerity," its pessimistic outlook does not quite square with the realities of the times.[63] Instead, Zoll perceives the nineteenth century as the apex of positivism and reductionism coupled with an individualistic atomism and selfish hedonism. At present he discerns that these forces are in retreat on some important fronts. A purely physical, mechanistic view of man is falling into disrepute today as people are becoming increasingly concerned with the question of quality and meaning in their lives. To Zoll the contemporary explosion of spiritual and psychological yearning would have been unthinkable a few short decades back. Humanity, especially in the Western world, is becoming aware that a purely physical manipulation of the way we live is not going to give us a will to live. Zoll therefore concludes that the prospects are good, if conservatives remain alert, for a reordering of society along rightist lines.

It is here, with his somewhat optimistic prognosis for the future, that Zoll finally parts company with the metaphysical conservatives. The God-fearing rightist would maintain, as L. Brent Bozell once put it, that it is impossible to order society rightly "without constant reference to God." Therefore, the religious conservative must look beyond our era and hope for some new dawn for mankind, while the empirical conservative can harbor some hopes for the here-and-now.

It would seem that empirical conservatism is doomed to remain the possession of an elite. Its naturalistic orientation would seem incapable, in the long run, of satisfying the psychological needs of most men. If what Zoll calls "the human social ethic" is in the final analysis nothing more than "universal motifs" and "natural obligations" that "must be transliterated into forms, symbolic and verbal, that are cognizable to human apprehension,"[64] then for the majority it would seem that satisfaction is only possible through self-deception. One must act *as if* religion, mythopoeticism, patriotism, familial and communal ties, and so on were real, when in

74

fact they are nothing more than a vitalistic symbolization of purely naturalistic wants and needs. Zoll does not shrink from these implications. He frankly describes empirical conservatism as "paternalistic" and sees its role as that of an intellectual vanguard, not a mass movement.[65]

We can now sum up the basic teachings of empirical conservatism. Like the metaphysical conservative, the empirical conservative is in deep disagreement with relativists and ideologues. Beginning with a concept of man as a creation of nature with certain transcultural and noncognitive, nonrational needs, wants, and faults, he rejects the simple formulations of relativism and its vision of man as an atomistic entity without any inherent values. This, the empirical conservative holds, is a dangerous distortion of man's actual makeup. Further, the empirical conservative, who generally adopts some form of "the civic ethic," as Zoll dubs it, cannot accept the situational subjectivism that is a central element of leftist relativism. That morality is binding on all is readily acknowledged by the empirical conservative, not, of course, because it is God's law, but because adherence to it is necessary for the communal existence of man and for the satisfaction of the psychological needs of man as an individual. Thus, the empirical conservative is at war with all forms of leftist amoralism as preached by positivists, reductionists, subjectivists, and relativists. His arsenal in this battle is not the Natural Law but nature's laws, or as we shall term them for our present purposes, *transrational truths*.

Equally anathema to the empirical conservative are the fanciful projections of ideology, the second heresy of the Left. The ideologue refuses to acknowledge the unchanging constitution of the human condition. He is the direct antithesis of the skeptical conservative with his no-nonsense view of mankind's aspirations and limitations, which have remained essentially constant throughout history.

Empirical conservatism teaches that the well-being of society is rooted in a clear recognition of the nature of man. An aberrational community is one that seeks to constitute itself in a manner contrary to the ethical and symbolic demands of its citizenry. Zoll, for example, faults American society at present for its inability to satisfy the basic needs of the individual, which he says fall under four broad headings:

1. peace . . . preeminently, internal domestic peace; 2. security —to be reasonably free in his immediate satisfaction from

external transgression; 3. to be liberated from frustration—to be allowed to attain and enjoy the fruits of his skill, industry and patience; 4. to be able to gain self-realization—to be treated as a person and not as a thing and to feel that *his* individuality and self-cultivation will merit effective justice.[66]

At bottom, then, the empirical conservative's diagnosis of and Rx for our present maladies are similar to those of the metaphysical conservative. He recognizes the timeless needs of man and seeks to fulfill these needs in ways that the strictly cognitive reductionist would find irrelevant. In summation we can say that *the empirical conservative rejects relativism and ideology on the basis of transrational truths, which he seeks to translate into the practical realm through moral sanctions, myths, and symbols that relate to the human situation.*

The Historical Conservative

Russell Kirk, noted author and a major theoretician of the post-war rightist resurgence, will be the subject of our examination of the doctrines of historical conservatism. In contrast to both Wilhelmsen and Zoll, whose writings draw upon a wide historical and geographical range of conservative thinkers, Kirk relies almost entirely upon the Anglo-American tradition. Kirk's distillation of conservative thought since Edmund Burke in *The Conservative Mind* excludes continental European conservatives with the terse comment that the subject is "too intricate for treatment here." The interest of the curious reader is naturally aroused: why, in a book that analyzes some thirty-odd conservative thinkers from Orestes Brownson to Henry Adams, and about eleven totally different forms of conservatism, running close to five hundred pages, could not some space have been found for a treatment of European conservatism? Indeed, one searches in vain throughout the remainder of Kirk's writings for any serious discussion of conservatism outside the Anglo-American tradition. At first glance Kirk seems to veer perilously close to the provincialist conservatism of the Evans-Meyer variety.

But Kirk's conservatism, although it nurtures itself on the Anglo-American tradition, does not equate the outward forms of that tradition with rightism proper. Consequently, the theories that

Kirk advances are for the most part universalist and transcend national and cultural boundaries, although the original sources of these theories are quite limited. As we quoted from Wilhelmsen previously, conservatives must grant their theoreticians certain "existential or historical preferences," while bearing in mind that the first principles of these men are of paramount importance. Russell Kirk the Tory conservative is really Russell Kirk the conservative, who happens to have derived his theories from the Tories.

It is not an easy task to present a short summary of Kirk's historical conservatism, for the simple reason that his rightism is a wide-ranging affair that encompasses many divergent philosophies. At times Kirk appears as a metaphysical or empirical conservative, bringing God and naturalistic data into his system. Here, however, we will study Russell Kirk as a historical conservative, advocating the value of ancestral wisdom, time-honored tradition, "prejudice," etc. This does not represent a distortion or limitation of his thought, for Kirk consistently presents the doctrines and apologetics of historical conservatism as capable of standing alone without the religious or realist justifications that sometimes go along with them. Kirk's historical conservatism is not the totality of his system, but it is a large and discrete part of it.

Before we begin it should be noted that Russell Kirk tends to view conservatism in general as an organic, rather mobile system of thought. "Conservatism is not a fixed and immutable body of dogma, and conservatives inherit from Burke a talent for reexpressing their convictions to fit the time," he writes.[67] Statements such as these abound in Kirk's works and they typify the Tory aversion for clearly spelled-out philosophical constructions. However, despite the disclaimer Kirk does find it possible to state a "working premise" about the "essence of social conservatism." It is "preservation of the ancient moral traditions of humanity. Conservatives respect the wisdom of their ancestors ... they are dubious of wholesale alteration." Nonetheless, according to Kirk, conservatives are not simply blind followers of earlier traditions, but support "reform" as opposed to "change." Kirk explains the difference between good and bad change when he writes:

> Society must alter, for slow change is the means of its conservation, like the human body's perpetual renewal; but Providence is the proper instrument for change and the test of a statesman is his cognizance of the real tendency of Providential social forces.[68]

To Kirk, the conservative is one who feels that "the wisdom of our ancestors" is a "trustier" guide to social welfare than reason, impulse, and materialistic determinism.[69] Why is Kirk so convinced that ancestral wisdom is more reliable than reason? Paraphrasing Edmund Burke, Kirk explains his position:

> Providence [has] taught humanity through thousands of years' experience and meditation, a collective wisdom; tradition, tempered by expedience. A man should be governed in his necessary decisions by a decent respect for the customs of mankind . . . The individual is foolish but the species is wise; prejudices and prescriptions and presumptions are the instruments which the wisdom of the species employs to safeguard man against his own passions and appetites . . . even the most intelligent of men cannot hope to understand all the secrets of traditional morals and social arrangements; but we may be sure that Providence acting through the medium of human trial and error, has developed every hoary habit for some important purpose . . . Prejudice is prejudgement, the answer with which intuition and ancestral consensus of opinion supply a man when he lacks either time or knowledge to arrive at a decision predicated upon pure reason.[70]

The translation of historical conservatism into the practical realm is beset with immense difficulties. Kirk bestows upon time-honored "prejudices, prescriptions, and presumptions" a kind of divine stamp of approval, with history as opposed to revelation the source of truth. "Every hoary habit" has an important Providential purpose. Yet as we quoted earlier, Kirk feels that change must take place, but only when its source is Providential. The problems with this thesis are obvious. It provides no criteria for condemning an evil, albeit time-honored custom, no criteria for differentiating between Providential change and bad change, no criteria for establishing when enough "time or knowledge" is available to allow reason to challenge tradition, and so on. Kirk runs dangerously close to affirming as a historical conservative a form of determinism or relativism, by telling us that history should be our guide to the good and that *all* ancestral wisdom is trustworthy. Willmoore Kendall perceived this chink in Kirk's armor:

> Mr. Kirk's teaching on tradition is, on the face of it, an assertion of the very relativism and positivism that, in other contexts, he

abhors. For it is, on the face of it, a teaching about the role and binding force of tradition in societies-in-general, and what it says about societies-in-general is that they are all somehow based on an "eternal contract," which enjoins a moral and religious tradition which is and, one gathers, ought to be transmitted from generation to generation by the family and, one gathers again, the local equivalent of "churches" (presumably shrines in Japan, mosques in Turkey, and temples in ancient Greece). . . . Because it declares all traditions equal, [this teaching of Kirk's] reduces the American tradition to the level of, say, the tradition that will obtain in the Soviet Union once the latter has succeeded in getting the Russian family and the Russian churches into the business of transmitting Communist doctrine. Contemporary American conservatism, one of whose basic quarrels *must* be the quarrel with relativism and positivism *in all their forms,* must give the teaching a wide berth.[71]

One tends to feel that there is something of great significance missing from historical conservatism on the theoretical level. It simply will not suffice to point to tradition as a guide to truth unless truth itself is first defined in some satisfactory way. Kirk himself keeps warm in his philosophical bullpen the able righty relief hurler of traditional religious faith (which he calls upon quite often when his historical conservatism falters) and the tricky southpaw fireman of empirical conservatism (which he calls upon less frequently; see, however, *The Conservative Mind* [New York: Avon Books, 1968], pp. 46–47). Yet he persists in presenting historical conservatism as a philosophy that can stand alone without the support of either theology or natural data verifiable by reason.

(By the way, the fault here is in all probability not Kirk's. Edmund Burke, whose conservatism takes precedence over all others in Kirk's writings, also left himself open to the same charge of theoretical superficiality. Witness, for example, the perennial debate over the true nature of Burke's philosophy. On the one hand is Peter Stanlis, who maintains that Burke belongs in the tradition of Natural Law, while Donald Atwell Zoll places Burke in the vitalist camp of empirical conservatism. The truth of the matter as I see it, having no personal axe to grind on this subject, is that in Burke's writings one finds ample support for both metaphysical and empirical conservatism. It appears that the author of the *Reflections* never probed very deeply into the philosophical sources of his temperamental and instinctual conservatism. Kirk, following his worthy teacher, seems similarly unwilling to come to grips with his real reasons for being a conservative.)

Standing alone, Kirk's historical conservatism is a logically indefensible position. When cornered, the historical conservative, if he wishes to make his apologetic hold water, must opt for either metaphysical or empirical conservatism. This does not mean, though, that historical conservatism carries little weight in the real world, where the prime concern of most men is not with the philosophical underpinnings of their lives but rather with their families, their jobs, their religious beliefs and practices, etc. Indeed it may be the most potent force in the ordering of the common man's existence. Every human being is to a certain extent a historical conservative, influenced by the traditions of his faith, nation, culture, family, and even by his own earlier experiences in life. We are all traditionalists.

Furthermore, the tradition in which we function is not that of the Australian aborigines or the nomads of the Gobi Desert but of Western civilization and all that it stands for. So when Kirk or other Tory conservatives speak in lofty phrases about tradition and ancestral wisdom, we must take their musings with a grain of salt. They don't really mean to say that the "ancestral prejudice" of sacrificing children to Molech should have been continued. All they are asking is that we, the bearers of classical philosophy and revealed faith as the West has understood them, should remain loyal, in the instinctual, nonrational way that men generally are loyal, to this, *our* tradition. The key to understanding historical conservatism is the realization that it is a system that does not answer the question, "What is conservatism?" but the altogether different, though important question, "What, in practice, makes people conservatives?" To which the historical conservative answers, quite accurately, "Traditions, ancestral wisdom, prejudices." Pushed into a corner and asked, "On what basis do you justify this tradition of yours?" the historical conservative will generally reply by saying something like, "Because traditions are usually right." This answer is of course false. One could easily catalogue a whole slew of traditions that every Western historical conservative rejects out of hand. The correct answer that the historical conservative should give (but of course will not give, because he dislikes full-blown rational explanations of his instinctual yearnings) is not that traditions are right but that *Western tradition is right.* Here he will have to choose between metaphysical and empirical conservatism; the tradition is right either because it is true in an ultimate, eternal sense (with God or Natural Law underwriting it) or because it is true for us as functional Western men—our collective unconscious (Jung), the "wisdom of nations" (Maurras), or some similar naturalistic cause persuades us to accept it.

To define historical conservatism is thus redundant. If we press the matter, and it must be pressed in the current context, historical conservatism inevitably reduces itself to either metaphysical or empirical conservatism. Historical conservatism is a means by which rightism is preserved, safeguarded, and transmitted to future generations. Most important of all, it is the conservatism of the majority of men. For the sake of continuity, though, let us say in summation that *the historical conservative rejects relativism and ideology on the basis of traditional (Western) truths, which he seeks to translate into the practical realm through customs, established beliefs, ancestral mores, traditions, and prejudices.*

The Realist Conservative

The patient reader who has stuck with me to this point has probably sensed by now that the working definition of conservatism we sought earlier has basically been arrived at. Despite their differences, all three universalist schools of rightist thought that we have examined are united by their rejection of amoralism and ideology, and their acceptance of some transrational source of unchanging values, morals, and needs. On the philosophical level this is just about as far as similarities among conservatives can be traced. Any attempt to go further will bring up questions of God, Natural Law, and like matters, on which conservatives must follow their own separate paths. However, the feelings of affinity that conservatives have shown transcend national, cultural, and religious boundaries. They seem to be based not upon theological affirmations, but rather upon similar beliefs about the nature of man and society and the place of man in society. Conceptual agreement means that conservatives also tend to favor the same general policies in different historical and national contexts.

Few conservatives have been willing to recognize—and capitalize upon—this essential agreement among rightists. The doctrinaire metaphysician is disinclined to water down his purity by admitting that wisdom may be found among the Gentiles. He therefore fails to draw upon the anthropological, historical, and psychological advances of recent decades that have served to give credence to many of the basic postulates of traditionalist conservatism. In addition, the temptation to strive for all-or-nothing, that is, to preserve one's quixotic remnant of integral purists at the expense of tangible and important gains for society at large and society's faith, is all too prevalent among metaphysical conservatives. Americans can visualize this purist religious fantasy of certain continental European conservatives by thinking of those die-hard rightists who romantically defend conservative positions of fifty years ago, feeling that it is of greater consequence to call for repeal of the Fourteenth and Sixteenth Amendments, or for state nullification of the *Brown* decision, than it is to influence the country in any significant way. The totalist conservative, of which the unbending metaphysical conservative is only one example, is crippled by his tenacious commitment to first principles. He is unable to see that the only place where first principles don't get bruised and battered is in the dressing room, where all the "Os" block all the "Xes" and every play is a touchdown.

But in the real world of conflict we must scratch and improvise, give and take, in order to achieve a fair approximation of what we desire ideally. Since he is a perfectionist, the metaphysical conservative balks at joining forces with the provincialist or historical conservative. Their emphasis on national myths, laws, customs, folkways, heroes, and the like convinces him that they neglect the real issues, which to him are theological first, last, and always. The empirical or naturalist conservative is of course a mere heretic and a completely unsuitable ally. What the metaphysical conservative fails to realize is that his purism is simply the result of his siege mentality. He views himself as God's chosen in the midst of a dying civilization. The fact that he functions in a culture that is mostly antagonistic to his values forces him to strengthen his own zeal and piety. But the pure faith that burns in his soul, almost totally impervious to outside forces, is not the faith that a broadly traditional, homogeneous, organic, and developing religious society gives birth to.* On the contrary, religion has always flour-

---

*To continue to put this in American terms, let us think of the idyllic picture that our own rightist purists paint of pre-1913 or pre-1932 America.

82

ished in societies where provincialism, patriotism, and ancestral traditions of all sorts give it cultural backdrop, depth, and continuity. The reluctance of the purists to join forces with other like-minded rightists is due to their fantasy-tinged approach to the values they seek to defend. The metaphysical purity of these rightists has its place, perhaps, in helping us gain an understanding of what God requires of men as individuals but not as members of communities, where our goal is not the spiritual perfection of the land but the preservation of faith through social equilibrium.

Similarly, as we observed before, the provincialist and historical conservative are severely limited in their ability to field a successful conservative movement except under the most favorable of circumstances. They are so completely immersed in their own cultural and national inheritances that they are incapable of responding adequately to the demands of the times. In the late nineteenth century, for example, the prudent as opposed to the provincialist conservative would have seen that the demand for government activity in the areas of old-age and unemployment insurance, antitrust legislation, farm aid, child-labor laws, and the like was sweeping the nation and would eventually triumph. If conservatives had broken free from the provincialist-historical trap of defending the old order at any cost, the reforms could have been enacted within a framework of traditional conservative first principles, as the Populists, Progressives, and Bull Moosers had advocated and, indeed, as the British Conservative Party early in the century actually achieved. Instead, the provincialist urge won out, the American Right stuck with the McKinleys and Tafts, with the Hardings and Coolidges, and finally went over the falls into virtual oblivion with the Hoovers and the Landons. While remaining true to its pure Horatio Alger philosophy, the American Right allowed the era of social reform to be preempted by the Deweyite logical positivists and materialists who provided much of the philosophical framework for the New Deal.

The horrendous results of this Last Stand of the conservatives are too numerous to discuss at length. Briefly, though, the long hibernation of the American Right from 1932 to 1964 made possible the disastrous foreign policies of Presidents Roosevelt and Truman, the drastic change in the moral climate of the nation, and the discrediting of old-school patriotism. All of those things are directly traceable to the failure of the American Right in the first quarter of the century to maneuver creatively. When the opportunity to change tack presented itself in 1964, the Right frivolously decided, as did Alf Landon in 1936, to run against the New Deal. And the results paralleled those of the original attempt to question the assumptions of welfarism. Theoretical purism and provincialist obstinacy have prevented conservatives from recognizing their core of common beliefs and translating their theories into *effective* political action.

Professor Thomas Molnar, prolific author of books and articles on political, social, and religious thought, is a notable exception to this gloomy picture. He clearly recognizes the essential unity of conservative thought throughout history and regardless of national boundaries. In his writings he draws freely from diverse rightist sources that at first glance would appear to be at war with each other. However, Molnar does not seem disturbed by these outward differences between the thinkers he refers to. We find him, for example in his work *The Counter-Revolution,* building upon the metaphysical conservatism of a Donoso Cortes, the legitimist-restorationist conservatism of a Joseph de Maistre, the Tory conservatism of an Edmund Burke, the theocratic-obscurantist conservatism of a Konstantin Pobiedonostsev, the empirical conservatism of a Charles Maurras, the republican-pluralist conservatism of a Willmoore Kendall, the nationalist conservatism of a José Antonio Primo de Rivera, and the democracy-admiring conservatism of Alexis de Tocqueville. Molnar sees no inconsistency in bringing together such an apparently heterogeneous group because he is well aware that

> the substance of counter-revolutionary affirmation . . . forms a rather straight line from the earliest counter-revolutionaries, such as de Maistre and Burke, to those of the 1930s and our own days.[72]

Donald Atwell Zoll, among others, has noted Molnar's ability to penetrate beyond the conflicting views of various segments of the Right and to pinpoint the continuity of conservative thought:

> Professor Molnar . . . avoid[s] . . . the *parochial,* the refusal to consider the problems of social remedy except within the narrow confines of some self-identified national tradition. The evaluation of ideological and political alternatives is certainly limited, in any rational sense, by historical and cultural factors, but the task of making efficacious recommendations can-

84

not be adequately accomplished by assuming a stance of philosophical and even political insularity and nationalistic
hubris.[73]

Besides transcending national and historical differences—which
is almost unique among contemporary American conservatives—
Molnar also makes generous use of recent advances in the fields of
anthropology, mythopoeticism, and psychology. He finds the
studies quite significant because they

> insist on the continuity of the human experience, of the sub-
> stratum variously symbolized but constantly present.[74]

To the conservative theoretician, the probing of history and its
various social constructions can yield ample support for two postulates to which the Right has long subscribed. As Molnar puts it:

> . . . first . . . they bear witness to the valuative processes
> inherent in man's make-up; and second, because they confirm
> the thesis of a common human experience, hence of this expe-
> rience as a historical and speculative norm.[75]

In Molnar we have discovered a rightist thinker who realizes that
conservatism is not bound by time or culture and that its basic
assumptions can be defended both empirically and metaphysically.
But Molnar's full contribution to rightism does not by any means
stop here. The no-nonsense realism that enables him to step ahead
of the provincialists and to marshal a host of original arguments for
the rightist cause is not limited to the realm of theory, but strongly
influences his thinking on practical matters as well. Indeed, it is in
this field of applied conservatism that Molnar's theories just may
be what the doctor ordered for the American Right.

To understand the realist conservatism of Molnar it is necessary
first to recognize that he is in essence what we have described
before as a metaphysical conservative. He feels that "the counter-
revolution has its deepest roots in religion."[76] Thus, when he
writes that behind the visible world lies

> *a real substratum* which thought is able to perceive, express,
> and act upon, although never in a perfect and definitive man-
> ner...

he hastens to add that this "substratum" has

> its roots in a transcendental system of reference, and that in
> fact this is why it is neither haphazard nor illusory.[77]

Despite (or perhaps, as we shall argue later, because of) his complete commitment to the truthfulness of metaphysical first principles, Molnar remains forever the realist. He cautions against a fanciful misconception of life's realities and warns that rightists should not "go about chasing illusions that we are always pure, and always dealing with pure situations." He urges conservatives to take note of the fact that "the world is made up of less than ideal conditions" and that as communal beings men must learn that "purity has often to be sacrificed for reasonable advantages here and now."[78]

Translated into practical terms this realism leads Molnar to endorse, for example, the change that the European Right opted for in the post–World War I period by advocating corporate nationalism as opposed to its earlier position, which called for some form of monarchial restoration. He writes:

> . . . the great question before counter-revolutionaries in modern times has been the reunification of the nation. As long as monarchies existed, in the nineteenth century, monarchy remained the obvious and ideal solution, and was to remain so even deep into the twentieth century. Yet the monarchic principle underwent subtle metamorphoses in the counter-revolutionary mind as it became clearer that nations split by ideologies and passions of class would accept a king either only as a figurehead or as the embodiment of a temporary, therefore precarious, ideological compromise . . .
>
> This explains why counter-revolutionaries began thinking of a different solution; the new formulation, increasingly popular as time went by, was that the nation must be reunited, made to commune in one "national faith" *before* it might receive the king. For this reason the monarchic principle itself had to be reinterpreted so as to mean only "national faith," temporarily incarnated in the rule of one man who is not king.[79]

In like manner Molnar believes that the papal condemnation of Action Française in 1926 was a "grave error" and that "benign neglect would have been the prudent course" at that time for the ecclesiastical authorities. Of course, Molnar is fully aware of the errors and gaps in Maurrassian theory, but he also realizes that on the whole the movement was an immense force for good in France in the political, social, and religious realms. (In fact, it was in its earlier years a wellspring of conversions to the Church.) Since man is constitutionally unable to know or foresee all things, Molnar concludes, he must opt for the greatest good he can conceive of under the circumstances. "Metaphysical *purity* has often to be sacrificed for reasonable advantages here and now."

At first glance this may seem to be at best a half-hearted policy of compromise or at worst some form of Machiavellian amoralism. But the accusation will not hold water. In the first place, Molnar has never advocated that conservatives compromise on their fundamental values and first principles. His policy of realistic maneuverability does not extend to the core of conservative metaphysical or empirical principles. Apart from these basics, though, Molnar feels that conservatives should let the virtue of prudence govern their actions. That is to say, they should keep their options open and operate as the realities of the times dictate. However—and this is one of the crucial points where Molnar parts company with the merely cynical, opportunistic *real politician*—he knows that this realistic approach to practical rightism is conceivable only if the rightists who follow it are firmly committed to, and clearly understand, their own first principles. Prudence can guide the conservative only if half of his heart is *not* already "on the other side." For example, Molnar has often been highly critical of Louis XVI and Nicholas II for their conciliatory attitude toward the insurrectionists of 1789 and 1917. He accuses them of "putting dignity and noble sentiments before the efficacy that the moment so imperatively demanded."[80]

Realist conservatism is therefore by no means a vague call to the sort of "muddling through" patchwork rightism that is frequently associated with Tory conservatives. Quite the contrary; it is a stark realization that the stakes involved in the rightist-leftist struggle are so high that it would be criminal negligence to let our personal preferences for ephemeral purities, meaningless forms, propagandistic phrases, and irrelevant moralisms blind us to the crying needs of the hour. Conservatives cannot afford to leave any stone unturned or any angle untried as they seek to insure the survival of order, community, and ultimately faith, for as rightists often lament, the hour is very, very late.

Typical of Molnar's realism-rooted-in-commitment is his position on Vatican contacts with Communist governments. He favors such exchanges, but not in the prevailing sense of worthless and, indeed, sinful dialogues, ecumenical exchanges of ideas, and the like. Obviously, contacts of this nature must not be pursued in a manner that would enhance the prestige of these tyrannical regimes and legitimate them in the eyes of their subject peoples. Rome can reap benefits from East-West contacts for the cause of faith the world over, but *only* if it employs wisdom and skill to further its own first principles. It must approach the matter without utopian fantasies about world peace or union, and with an eye open to the realities of practical politics. A similar situation exists in the case of America's participation in the United Nations. Membership in that world body could hold great diplomatic and propagandistic potential if the United States would only remain firmly committed to its own goals and ideals. At present, incidentally, it appears that neither Rome nor America is able or willing to follow such policies.

As for the second criticism mentioned above—that a certain degree of amoral Machiavellianism seems to infect Molnar's philosophy—it should be stressed that Molnar's realism does not run counter to the theological foundations of his thinking. Evil acts of a cruel or illicit nature are not part of the conservative repertoire. Molnar's realistic beliefs can be summarized in three short statements:

1) Conservative principles should not be confused with the passing forms with which rightism garbs itself in different contexts and times. This point recurs in Wilhelmsen's and Zoll's systems as well.

2) Prudence or realism should be our guide when changing forms and seeking to maintain the basic conservative beliefs. Rightists fight, compromise, propagandize, educate, retreat, electioneer, and so on with one central ambition: to preserve the conservative assumptions that must, morally and empirically, underlie every society. Here Molnar's theories are slightly, but significantly, different from those of Wilhelmsen, who only belatedly abandons the symbols of an older conservative order when he finds them already defeated, hoping then to "sacramentalize" the new order; and Zoll, who only seems to say that conservatives must keep step with the demands of the populace. Molnar, on the other hand, supplies us with a somewhat different criterion. Conservatives enter the temporal order to stabilize it through application of rightist truths.

88

Their only goal is to secure practical advantages for their side, which means that sometimes they move with history's currents, at other times they fight them, at other times they ignore them, and so on.

3) Tangible gains for conservatism can only be achieved by employing, in each sphere of human activity, methods that work. Diplomacy, education, politics, religion, law enforcement, and other areas all have their own special procedures for achieving success. Only in regard to this last point does any question of amoralism enter into the picture. Conservatives may legitimately disagree here, and of course they do. However, Molnar's major contribution as a rightist thinker is his ability to discern that in order to move forward conservatives must learn and exploit the methodology of every realm of society. All religious faiths in their orthodox incarnations recognize that the business of governing families, schools, communities, and countries calls for the application of a framework of values that sometimes differs from that of the purely individual life. The exact time, place, and reason for such deviations are matters that theologians—and conservatives—debate among themselves, but the fact that deviations must occasionally take place is universally admitted.

One final aspect of Molnar's thought is important in this context. In oppositon to Wilhelmsen, who sees the ultimate goal of communal endeavor as the "sacramentalization of being," Molnar suggests much less perfectionist aims for the conservative cause. Zoll comes closer to Molnar's view when he posits, as the end purpose of rightism, the restoration of a "civic ethic" and the satisfaction of man's natural needs, including relief from abnormal fears or frustrations. Translating these broad statements into specific guidelines, Molnar feels that conservatism's ultimate purpose is "nonspectacular"; it is, simply stated, to "defend society and the principles of ordered community."[81] The rightist seeks merely to follow "society's natural rhythm" and to establish a "harmony that links community and citizen, government and nation, past and present, history and the future." This can be done only when "social peace, careful and minimal lawbreaking, and protection against upheavals"[82] are the foundations of the realm. Molnar realizes, of course, that organic communities of this sort can function only when there is a transcendental substratum presupposed by the people and their leaders.

Molnar's conservatism rounds out our search for the essence of rightism. It rejects amoralism and ideology, but on the basis of *both* empirical *and* metaphysical notions. It acknowledges that the truths of being must be incarnated in various traditions, mythopoetic forms, and the like. It does not, however, advocate that rightists proceed in a vacuum, ignorant of outside forces and influences, and it cautions that they must employ the methods and means of this world to achieve real advantages in it. Molnar's conservatism provides a firm link between theory and practice, thought and deed. Pointing to the fact that God has enjoined man to live in an imperfect world, it concludes that men of the Right must seek to protect and advance their first principles in an empirically realistic manner.

We have thus arrived at a definition of conservatism that provides a philosophical framework for dealing with the actual situations that we will shortly be examining. Before moving on to practical politics, however, we must train our sights on America and investigate American conservatism in the light of the preceding definition. To remain a vital force, conservatism must take into account the cultural context in which it finds itself, but it must not mistake the cultural context for its own essence. What is conservatism in the American situation? That is the next question we must answer.

3 What Is American Conservatism?

Every nation that is not the creation of artificial political maneuvering has certain traditions that set the framework for the institutions functioning within it. These national traditions, rooted in the religious, mythical, and cultural nuances of a land and its people, are not arbitrary constructions that can be tampered with in a whimsical manner. The stability and indeed the very survival of society are largely based upon the degree to which it remains loyal to its heritage. Rightists, who are frequently referred to as traditionalists, have always recognized this truth. Expressing themselves with various degrees of refinement and understanding, conservatives have sought to advance the cause of the traditions they have inherited. One of the prime responsibilities of rightists in any given historical situation is to discover the true nature of their society's public past and its assumptions about man and life. Ultimately, they must seek to demonstrate the relevance of the past to the issues of the day.

As I noted before in discussing historical conservatism, not all traditions have equal claims to legitimacy. To take Kendall's example of the contemporary Soviet regime, it is obvious that even if the Communist totalitarianism currently in power in Russia should survive long enough to develop some of the outward forms of traditions, it would still not warrant our support. This is a point that conservatives (traditionalists) have sometimes missed. The rightist is often so preoccupied with presenting the argument that a community can function naturally only if it observes conservative first principles that he tends to forget that communities do at times function *unnaturally* under despotism, disregarding the normative requirements of social equilibrium. However successful a totalitarian regime may appear, though, and regardless of whether it flaunts the outward trappings of a national heritage, there are two fundamental reasons why its traditions can never be termed legitimate.

The first reason springs from the empirical substructure of conservative theory: to merit our approval, a tradition must not set itself in opposition to reality as we know it. The "final solutions" of leftist utopianism, with its projection of future bliss to be ushered in at some unspecified date by a "remade man" leading a paradisal existence, are completely incompatible with the needs of real-life societies, which require unifying beliefs and commitments to solidify their existence in the here-and-now. Any doctrine that negates the validity of human experience is at root merely another attempt magically to manipulate being, just as the ancient alchemists hoped to transform material substances. Utopian plans are doomed, ultimately, either to fail or to be enforced against the general wisdom and common good by police-state methods. Therefore, traditions emanating from totalitarian philosophies are not traditions in the true sense of the term. They can only be sustained by regimes that deny the citizenry their dignity as human beings. Such traditions must maintain their precarious hold on a frustrated populace by abnormal means.

The second reason why the traditions of totalitarianism are never legitimate arises from the metaphysical substructure of conservative thought: to merit our approval, a tradition must not contradict the eternal values upon which society is based. Value-free communities such as those envisioned by the theoreticians of relativism are sinful in their rejection of revealed and natural law, as well as unsuitable to the empirical demands of group existence. People cannot live in either personal or communal tranquility without some sort of moral frame of reference. The dogmas of relativism, which declare all questions open, all values subjective, and all norms illusory, would, if taken seriously, break down all communal structures. Therefore, the second criterion for a legitimate tradition is that it acknowledges the ultimacy of moral values.

Having set down these brief guidelines to what does *not* constitute tradition, we can now state the logical corollary: specifically, that all national, local, and ethnic traditions that operate within the two criteria are legitimate ways for Western man to symbolize the twin truths of empirical being and revelatory faith. However, the traditions of the West as they have been cast and recast in various societies are not static. They do change throughout the centuries. There is a distinct element of mobility, of progression and regression, in even the most harmoniously balanced societies. If we seriously hope to understand the traditions of our own country, we must first seek to understand the processes by which traditions in general may change but remain true to their essence. In short, we must have a workable conservative theory of change.

"What is American conservatism?" is thus in the final analysis a somewhat more detailed question in two parts: (1) How has our country over the years symbolized the first principles of conservatism? and (2) How have these symbols actually changed over the years? Later we shall turn our attention to a third question: Are there traditions still extant in contemporary America that communicate the essential core of Western truth?

If at this point I appear to be using the terms conservatism and traditionalism interchangeably, it is indeed my intention to do so. Conservatism is a form of wisdom. It realizes that finite men express weighty truths through temporal symbols, myths, attitudes, and customs—things familiar to the whole community. Americanism, as long as it remains faithful to the requirements of truth by rejecting relativism and by expressing values mythopoetically, is the only form of conservatism that can succeed in the United States. We cannot realistically hope to transfer the symbols of a different cultural context to our own shores, attempting thereby to imbue our system with the essences underlying those foreign symbols. One may feel, for example, as many conservatives do, that hereditary monarchy is an extremely appropriate symbol for expressing familial and hierarchical concepts. These feelings should not, however, blur one's view of the realities of our constitutional republic, its traditions, and the general mood of the American populace throughout history—all of which are decidedly against any sort of officially sanctioned hereditary rule. So, whatever the weak-

93

nesses of our American traditions, they remain, for better or worse, *our* traditions and it is within this framework that we must theorize. In sum, Americanism is the conservatism of an American.*

What Is Tradition?

What precisely do we mean when we speak of the traditions through which America symbolically depicts Western truth? Apparently we would not want to include mere customs in our definition of traditions, such as the white wigs and knee-length breeches that the Founding Fathers wore, or the public flogging of criminals, which was common practice at the nation's inception.** What, then, is a tradition?

A tradition is a group's image of itself. It is a symbol that tells how the group—a religious faith or an ethnic unit, or a village, city, or nation—views its continuity and cohesiveness; in short, how it views the significance of its existence. These self-images—traditions—are the product of many divergent influences in the public

*We may, of course, feel an emotional closeness to other conservative forms. But this attachment belongs on the level of inspirational support and philosophical enlightenment, not of practical imitation. The group of American Catholic traditionalists who took to wearing the red berets and Marian insignia of the Spanish Carlists might have deepened their own faith experience through such symbolization. Nonetheless, they could not reasonably have hoped thereby to reach Americans and reclaim their country for the very transcendental truths they so beautifully showed allegiance to.

**One hesitates to create the impression that the discontinuance of either of these practices is evidence of progress or refinement. The aristocratic dignity of the colonial gentleman was greatly enhanced by his dress. Ideally, this distinct form of dress was merely the outward manifestation of the honor, learning, and high ethical standards of the upper classes. Such customs should not be lightly discarded unless there are suitable cultural substitutes available. Similarly, in the case of flogging it would be interesting to see New York City, for example, put into practice a scheme I heard recently from a noted rightist thinker: that all criminals in the city convicted of violent crimes should, before commencing their sentences, be publicly flogged at high noon, at the site of the crime, after a week in which the flogging would be widely publicized at government expense in the major newspapers and on the local radio and television networks. The lashes would be administered by members of the local community selected at random. Would this be a step backward or a much needed Rx for the Big Apple?

94

past. Legends concerning the establishment of the group, beliefs about the nature of its members, and many similar things all play a part in constituting traditions. It is of little importance whether these traditions of the group are based upon actual historical occurrences; likewise, it makes little difference whether the assessment of the group character is based upon an empirically verifiable estimation of cultural attributes or is the result of popular prejudice. (That is, it makes little theoretical difference. On a practical level it is very difficult to maintain popular traditions that openly contradict the realities that the citizenry sees. For example, the Southern myth of white supremacy was kept alive only so long as the black people were rigidly segregated from society. In recent years it has lost its credibility.) The nature of human social life seems to demand that society, if it is not to degenerate to anarchy, share a generally acknowledged framework of beliefs, assumptions, and myths. These are known as traditions.

Eternal Values, Traditions, and Customs

We must of course distinguish on the one hand between eternal values and traditions, and on the other hand between traditions and customs. An eternal value is a truth of the human condition, ultimate and immutable, whether its source is divine revelation, Natural Law, or the "civic ethic." There are important differences here between a metaphysical rightist and his empirical counterpart on what would be an eternal value. For convenience let us focus on the theological conservative. To him an eternal value could be either a positive injunction, irreformable, like the sacraments in Catholicism and the commandments in Judaism, or a negative prohibition, such as those forbidding illicit sex, abortion, evil traits of character, and so on. A tradition, by contrast, is a symbolic form through which a group seeks to safeguard, transmit, and enhance an eternal value by relating it in some way to the needs and exigencies of this-worldly existence. Traditions are deeply ingrained in the public psyche and express themselves in broad, soul-satisfying terms capable of surving over long periods of time. Finally, customs are those outward physical symbols of a group—their manners, dress, recreations, rituals, speech, habits, celebrations and the like—which, although generally relating back to traditions and thus ultimately to eternal values, are transient and vary greatly from generation to generation.

I do not pretend to know why God created human beings to function on these three different levels. What is obvious, however, is that in fact this is how societies and individuals operate. To cite a purely religious example, let us look at prayer. Here the eternal value is simply that man should pray to God, thanking and entreating Him and accepting His Kingship over him. In reality, though, all religious groups develop intricate traditions that regulate how one should approach God in prayer. In the minds of the faithful these traditions become intermingled with the value itself. Then, in the final stage of development, communities establish their own unique customs regarding the form of prayer. This process of broadening, enriching, and symbolizing the eternal value of prayer is not a falsification. It is the way temporal man reacts to transcendence, making it comprehensible to him and relevant to his station in life. Prayerbooks, hymns, ecclesiastical architecture, candles, and other traditions and customs are not in themselves prayer, but they are the means whereby man makes prayer a meaningful part of his existence.

To cite another example of a more secular nature, let us take a theme from American history, the central importance of "the people" throughout the nation's existence. "The people" rise up against the excesses of the English crown; "We the people" establish the republic; our government is "of, by, and for the people"; or, in recent years, "the people" demand the two World Wars and "the people" force us to withdraw from Vietnam. Rarely in the Western world, except perhaps in revolutionary France, have "the people" been so highly exalted. Now, at first glance this adulation of "the people," as it expressed itself at the time of the American revolution and as it has continued to express itself in American history for two centuries, would seem to grow out of the same sort of amoral democratic theory with which relativism is associated. That is, a quasireligious faith in the will of "the people" to regulate the affairs of the nation. Taken literally, the primacy given to "the people" in America would seem to negate all eternal values and beliefs in favor of whatever happens to capture the national fancy at any moment. As a tradition, American democracy would not embody the themes of eternity but stand in stark contradiction to them.

96

However, a closer look at American democracy shows that our populist myths cannot be equated with those of democratic relativism. "The people" of the American tradition are not just any old people but a specific kind of people. They are presented in the mythopoetic realm as hard-working, family-loving, God-fearing, commonsensical folk. Moreover, it would be a virtually fruitless endeavor to search in the documents and writings of the founding of the American nation for statements that elevate "the people" above eternal norms or values. Indeed, for the overwhelming majority of the Founding Fathers "the people" are a relevant ideal only within the framework of some kind of religious or at least classical philosophic worldview. The maintenance of public virtue and communal order are always seen as preceding and remaining superior to the will of "the people." It would have been inconceivable to the men who founded America that their devotion to "the people" would be interpreted as something above or outside of the normative traditions of Western man. So the genesis of the American tradition of "the people" (and the genesis of a tradition is vitally important to its understanding) was in fact a belief in the *virtuous* people as bearers of the Western tradition.

Our American belief in "the people" is therefore a suitable example of a *tradition*. It qualifies as a tradition because it is part and parcel of the public past and of the contemporary assumptions about life to which all American leaders as a matter of rote pledge their unyielding allegiance, and because the citizenry at large considers it one of the basic foundations of communal existence. Deference to "the people" is not merely a custom. It is not an outward way of doing things and it could not be eliminated from the American scene without some kind of revolutionary tampering with the procedures of our society or some form of totalitarian suppression by forces determined to impose their will upon the populace. America minus its commitment to "the people" simply would not be the America that its own citizens know, or the America that the world in general knows.

"The people" is a legitimate tradition in line with the transcendent values. It is a symbol that articulates the eternal value of establishing a virtuous and orderly society. "The people" are viewed as good; they will cherish good things and defend against evil ones. Of course, we must remember that "the people" is essentially a myth that has at best a tenuous relation to the realities of American life. Suffrage was only extended to "the people" grad-

97

ually, and obviously the power of "the people" as opposed to that of the schools and the media is not terribly great. All of this is irrelevant, however. "The people" exists, reality notwithstanding! Recently the tradition of "the people" has been misrepresented so that at present it veers dangerously close to the heretical relativism of the ideological democrats. But as a symbolic ideal by which Americans can live and understand the pursuit of justice and morality, "the people" has over the years proved to be a highly workable Western tradition.

Social Change

Any discussion of values, traditions, and customs would be incomplete without a reference to the degree of permanence inherent in all three and the means whereby groups may or may not alter them.

In the area of values the conservative (and particularly the metaphysical conservative) simply cannot tolerate any degree of change or "reform." Conservatism teaches, if it teaches anything, that God, traditional morality, justice, human dignity, and the like cannot be changed or amended. This is the starting point for any theory of rightism. (Of course, at times prophets may arise, like the three major and twelve minor prophets of the Old Testament, who add to the main body of divine revelation. But the transcendental can *only* be tampered with in just such a supratemporal manner. Conservatives not inspired by the Holy Spirit must treat it as sacred ground.)

Traditions are a different kettle of fish. They are not, so to speak, *the thing itself;* they are its derivatives. However, their broad acceptance by the group and their close connection with eternal values in the group's psyche make the question of changing or reforming traditions an extremely complex and important one for conservatives. For the most part, alas, rightist thinkers have not truthfully confronted this problem. If, indeed, they touch on it at all, they do so in a hopelessly superficial manner by saying things like "Conservatives favor slow change but oppose radical change," or "Conservatives favor wise change but oppose flippant change," and so on. Statements such as these, while containing a kernel of truth, are almost completely untranslatable into the realm of practical politics.

98

The theoretical problem involved here requires close attention, for it affects the rightist position on a huge number of issues in any historical period. Conservative stances can usually be divided into four categories: (1) the advocacy of eternal values, as embodied in legislation like the Human Life Amendment or the antipornography statutes; (2) the advocacy of traditional symbolizations of values, such as opposition to the welfare state for McKinleyesque reasons (it breaks down the Protestant work ethic); (3) the defense of eternal values as symbolized in social customs (traditional morality in America sought at various times to forbid men's topless swimsuits, mixed bathing, the bikini, and so on); (4) prudential assessments of technical matters, such as the American Right's opposition to unbalanced budgets on the ground that deficit financing would ruin the economy. The question of conservatism and change has direct bearing on categories two and three.*

*I have set up the fourth category in deference to American conservatism as it exists today. Only economists and mathematicians differ over balanced budgets, not rightists and leftists. There is nothing inherently liberal about inflation. Whether inflation stimulates the economy is a question of economic theory, nothing more. Unfortunately, in America these obvious facts are shrouded in a mist of tradition and custom. As a result, the Right's defense of balanced budgets is caught up in various traditions of states' rights, individualism, and the Protestant work ethic. Recently, though, conservatives have been sticking to empirical apologetics here. The issue is therefore in a state of flux.

From a conservative standpoint, any economic system is legitimate if it does not advocate the abolition of private property or, on the other side of the spectrum, condemn any and all charitable efforts by government as a matter of principle. An economic system may be unwise. But this does not make it rightist or leftist.

The defense of private property must remain an important part of the conservative program because both traditional Western religion and an empirical assessment of the needs of man testify to its importance. The form in which the institution of private property is maintained may of course vary greatly. Thus, despite the fact that Russell Kirk in The Conservative Mind seeks to deny the conservative credentials of G.K. Chesterton and Hilaire Belloc because they advocated distributism, it should be clear that conservatives, too, can favor land reform. The conservative, who wishes to lessen wherever he can the anomic frustrations of modernity, should be alert to new ways of providing mankind with the feelings of satisfaction that home and land bring. Again, distributism may have been impractical, but it was certainly far from being antithetical to conservatism. Doctrinaire libertarianism, on the other hand, is inherently leftist; see the footnote on page 67.

To the extent that activist conservative publications such as National

Once again we must differentiate between values and traditions (or customs). I dwell on this point, probably to the exasperation of the reader, because conservatives so frequently misunderstand it and in consequence severely hurt the movement. Conservatives, for the life of them, can't seem to understand that a tradition is not and cannot become an eternal value. To illustrate this confusion, let us look at the reason contemporary conservatives give for their opposition to the Women's Liberation movement in general and to its main legislative goal, the Equal Rights Amendment, in particular. I do hope it is unnecessary to document the fact that rightist concern over the ERA is not really based upon the constitutional and practical problems foreseen in its implementation, of which we read so much in activist conservative publications. These arguments are of course handy debating points when employed for their polemical value; they are not the source of the rightist position, which is, obviously, a traditionalist allegiance to the family structure as we have inherited it and as orthodox faith has generally portrayed it.

When presenting the traditionalist case against the ERA conservatives invariably say something like, "The ERA will destroy or seriously weaken the family as we know it." Translated into intelligible theoretical terms, the argument runs as follows: "There is a human institution known as the family. We 'know' of it in a certain way from divine revelation, Natural Law, empirical data, etc. The ERA will destroy or seriously weaken this institution." Historical perspective might counsel against making such sweeping arguments. Indeed, this very form of polemic has been used many times in world history. Rightists have used it to describe the "terrible" effects of the Seventeenth Amendment, of women pursuing careers in the marketplace, of mixed schooling, and if we turn the clock

---

Review and *Human Events* must deal with the practical issues of daily politics, they will inevitably comment on a number of merely pragmatic economic questions. There is nothing wrong with conservatives' saying that deficit spending will raise the cost of living or that certain federal programs are so inefficiently administered that huge numbers of ineligibles are allowed to participate, to cite two examples that American rightists harp on. However, these concerns could equally interest a sincere (as opposed to a party-line) leftist. We need only think of Senator William Proxmire to remind ourselves of this. The American Right must remember (and this is a point that will be discussed at length in the following chapters) that however important it may be to get the minimum wage repealed, it is far more important to see that America readopts the central teachings of conservatism concerning God, man, and community.

back far enough, we will find the traditionalist elements in society opposing education for women altogether. Clearly, though, none of the reforms just mentioned has destroyed, weakened, or even altered those families which have remained loyal to the eternal values that underlie the institution of the family. Thus, it would appear that it is not the change itself that threatens the family, but the mood that surrounds the change in the public mind. That is to say, while in 1910 those advocating women's suffrage were, for the most part, not as concerned about the preservation of the Judeo-Christian family as were their opponents, by 1978 it makes no difference to millions of traditional Protestant, Catholic, and Jewish housewives whether or not they have the right to vote. In retrospect it would seem that the women's-suffrage movement was not a danger in itself, but only because it symbolically incarnated certain trends of thought that were potentially damaging. However, the conservatives of that era did not grasp this and so they viewed the Seventeenth Amendment as a direct attack on the family structure of the West.

In truth, what conservatives should have said* at the time was, "The fact that women do not vote in American society is a custom through which we seek to revere and uphold the paternal society, a tradition of our nation that has as its basis the Judeo-Christian value of family life. If you leftists should succeed in doing away with this custom, you will not destroy our paternalistic tradition, or the traditional Western family values. Fortunately, we possess many other customs and traditions through which we express the ideals in which we believe. In fact, until you turn your fire on the divinely ordained concepts of chaste and monogamous marriage between male and female, of the right and duty of parents to bear and raise their own children, and of the hierarchical structure of the family with parents as the source of authority, deserving of respect from their offspring, you will not even have begun to touch our real values, our eternal values. You will rob us, however, of the joy and contentment we derive from the many symbolizations of these val-

---

*By "should have said" I mean, of course, should have understood as a matter of theoretical clarity. It seems, however, that the majority of Americans, or at least of community activists, like to have their politics served up with generous helpings of Armageddon-type rhetoric. I do not mean to imply that the 1910 equivalents of *Human Events* and *Battle Line* should not have propagandized as they did, only that conservative thinkers should have had a better grip on what was truly at stake.

ues." Of course, as the Left continues, generation after generation in country after country, to destroy the myriad traditions through which Western man has symbolized the transcendental values of his life, the values themselves become endangered because the people can no longer celebrate, symbolize, and therefore *remember* the essential norms that they profess.

Traditions and Change

Traditions are not as basic as values. By definition they are the cultural, national, or religious symbolizations of the substratum of eternal truths and empirical realities. They are therefore not immutable. Nevertheless, because of the reality of the public past, because of the national consciousness and the sense of community, traditions cannot be discarded or changed or even added to with impunity. The question thus confronts us how and when traditions may change without damaging the social fabric or weakening the eternal values called into question by the proposed reform. We will also examine the related question when, if ever, conservatives should actually be in the vanguard of reform.

At the outset conservatives must realize that these questions do not apply to attempts to change traditions grounded in amoral or immoral philosophies like relativism, Communism, and Nazism. All such systems must be viewed as illegitimate from the conservative perspective. Having said this, though, we must turn our attention to several other areas of social change.

Evil Traditions

Not all traditions, even those of societies that function within the framework of Western values and empirical realism, are good or beneficial. The tendency among European conservatives to idolize each and every institution of the *ancien régime,* or among American conservatives fancifully to portray pre-1932, 1913, 1861, 1824, or 1800 America, has become exaggerated of late, with the Right beginning to see itself in many countries as a doomed sect of nostalgiacs romantically yearning for some mythical past. These fantasies, however understandable from an emotional standpoint, are obviously nurtured on a false, almost utopian vision of traditional societies. Flawed and fallible man is never free from his natural penchant to err and sin, despite the basic soundness of his theoretical first principles and of the communal structure in which he lives. As a result, even the most ideally ordered of realms will inevitably produce customs and occasionally even traditions that are either evil or impossibly unworkable.

An example of an institution that arose in the orthodox religious atmosphere of the Middle Ages and nevertheless resorted to evil methods to carry out its mission would be the Inquisition, which in various countries used torture and blackmail to extract evidence and confessions. The use of torture is properly described not as a tradition but as a custom. Yet torture was accepted by what may be described as the extreme Inquisitionist tradition, which flouted the eternal values of justice and brutally demeaned the dignity of man in an attempt to reach justifiable goals. (Of course, the normative Inquisitionist tradition, which desired to safeguard the populace from what it considered to be the dangers of heresy by employing legitimate legislative and executive means, and at times even sought to convert unbelievers through persuasion to the religion of the majority, was a true conservative Western tradition. I do not imply, however, that some form of theistically oriented pluralist society is not equally legitimate, for it certainly is.) Sincere conservatives living at that period in history would have been obligated to seek, to the best of their abilities, to eliminate the extreme Inquisitionist tradition from their societies.

Another tradition that was popular toward the end of the *ancien régime,* especially in France, was the theory of absolute monarchy, with centralization of power in the national government. The various theoreticians (conservative, of course) who advanced these proposals were ignoring the empirically demonstrable need for a nation to be subdivided into local autonomous groupings—geographical, ethnic, or familial. These divisions were organically developed in the Catholic Middle Ages and provided a suitable balance between the demands of liberty and those of community. The absolutists brushed aside the realities of the situation and ultimately worked untold harm upon the very monarchial structure that they tried in their zeal to uphold artificially. True conservatives would have fought this new tradition because it was contrary to the demands of man and community.

Thus we see that conservatives are not bound to defend all customs and traditions that originate in Western cultures. They owe prior allegiance to the practical realities of the human situation and to the demands of God. At times conservatives are actually obligated to lead the effort to eliminate certain traditions of an evil or errant nature.

Imperfect Traditions

What should be the conservative reaction to a tradition that, while striving to articulate an eternal value, in reality inaccurately represents it or distorts it? To pursue this question, I have selected the tradition of feudalism or, more specifically, serfdom as it existed in czarist Russia before 1861.

Serfdom was a system rooted in the aristocratic doctrines of the Middle Ages, which subscribed strongly to the importance of hierarchical distinctions based upon ancestry, wealth, property, and education. To the modern mind, conditioned by the dogmas of egalitarianism, the mere mention of social classes and distinctions is anathema. Unfortunately, it is not within the scope of this volume to enter into a lengthy presentation of what may be called "aristocratic apologetics." In passing, though, let us note that the deferential society where respect and humility, personal honor and familial attachments, were expected from the several social strata, beginning with kings, archdukes, and princes and ending with commoners and serfs, with all ultimately deferring to God, furnished the citizenry with a profound sensibility to innumerable moral virtues. In addition, it was felt that a hereditary and landed aristocracy would give society a source of stability and continuity. Moreover, it was hoped that the elite classes would play an important role in transmitting culture and morals, although, of course, the reality all too frequently did not live up to the ideal.

There are obvious faults in the system of hereditary aristocracy. The deferential society does not provide much of an opportunity for a capable and deserving man at the bottom to move to the top. Perhaps the hierarchical groupings tended to frustrate some of the natural yearnings, talents, and ambitions of the populace. But whatever the relative merits of the deferential society, it should be pointed out that the system did not emerge out of the blue. To work, it must have had the community's assent, that is, true organic assent deriving from the deep-seated beliefs, assumptions, myths, and prejudices of the public past and contemporary national consciousness. All in all, hereditary and landed class distinctions would appear to be in certain cultural and religious circumstances a legitimate means of expressing some of the basic values of Western man. Aristocracy is an imperfect system, but then again, such is the nature of all men and institutions.

Aristocracy does not of necessity imply a system of feudal slavery or serfdom. However, in the early Middle Ages throughout Catholic Europe and until a century ago in Russia, that was in fact the way the system manifested itself. Various forms of slavery had, of course, been part and parcel of social life from time immemorial. The Old Testament seems to condone it, as did most of the leading philosophers of classical Greece. The questions that confront conservatives here are the same that Alexander II wrestled with before he liberated the Russian serfs in 1861: Is the dignity of the serf as a human being so degraded by his lowly stature as to warrant abolishing the system? Is serfdom too extreme a form of the traditional Western attempt to symbolize the hierarchy of values through hierarchical social structures? Furthermore, could society withstand the strain on its social cohesiveness that the rapid abolition of serfdom would undoubtedly impose? (It is all too easy for twentieth-century conservatives, especially American rightists, to declare pompously that serfdom is under any and all circumstances and in any and all societies evil. In our own country the traditions associated with independence and individualism are too strong for us to appreciate the deferential society in general and feudalism in particular.)

To resolve this perplexing dilemma, conservatives should finally have recourse to their old ally, prudence. Serfdom has in fact been practiced in different ways, with different methods, and consequently with different results. In recent years American slavery, for example, has been interpreted in terms ranging from the highly favorable to the strongly condemnatory. There would seem to be no set of *a priori* standards here. A conservative would have to examine whatever practice of serfdom might exist in his own country and draw his own conclusions whether the individuals in question were being denied the basic dignities of beings created in the image of God. The guideline here is prudence, a prudential assessment of the realities of serfdom in a given time and place.

We see, then, that a legitimate tradition may endanger the eternal values conservatives seek to defend. A serfdom that brutalizes and humiliates the serf, as opposed to loving and caring for him, is such a case. In these situations the conservative must not allow his emotional attachment to the old order to blind him to his central duty. The rightist must seek to change distorted traditions with the same zeal with which he defends the good ones. Indeed, it has been precisely this failure of the Right to display a morally grounded social consciousness—its natural possession—that has gravely damaged the conservative image in the public mind.

One final consideration must be borne in mind when speaking of the conservative's opposition to certain traditions and his advocacy of social reform. The rightist is not an ideologue. He does not legislate his morality in a contextual vacuum. Konstantin Pobiedonostsev always claimed that Alexander II's freeing of the serfs was a significant factor in the revolutionary ferment that pervaded nineteenth-century Russia, leading to Alexander's assassination and culminating in the revolution that Pobiedonostsev foresaw but did not live to see. If this analysis is correct, the prudential conservative would not have wanted to abolish serfdom without channeling the new freemen into normative society through proper religious, educational, and economic policies.

Conservative Innovation

We have just spoken of conservative change in the sense that rightists seek to abolish or reform traditions and traditional institutions that fail to fulfill their purpose. There is another type of change in society that is often referred to as reform, but could be more adequately described as innovation.

By innovation I mean a new tradition or custom introduced into society that not only affects a specific area but alters society's previous assumptions. The huge welfare-state apparatus erected in America at the time of the New Deal did not merely alleviate the pain of the Depression; it represented a break with the capitalist, individualist, Protestant-work-ethic tradition generally associated with the Republican Party of that period. Today, of course, the welfare state is taken for granted. Even the Right no longer opposes (actively, anyway) the basic principle that motivated the New Deal, namely, that when individuals cannot obtain through the private sector the basic necessities and securities of life, it behooves the government step in and help. For all practical purposes, the extreme individualism of the McKinley-Coolidge-Hoover type has

106

been abandoned; a tradition has been set aside. For conservatives this situation provides ample opportunity to examine the process whereby brand-new traditions are introduced into the public mind.

The free-enterprise tradition in America was what we have defined heretofore as a legitimate tradition. It emphasized the important values of personal responsibility, honor, devotion to family, local autonomy, and other commendable virtues. However, it also encouraged a certain amount of selfishness. It sometimes denied or belittled the natural humane sympathies that are so important in communal situations, and it failed to satisfy the psychological needs of the urban working class. Still, it was one of the ways in which a late nineteenth-century America sought to incarnate the eternal values.

This tradition was challenged in the American context by four attempts to introduce a new tradition in its place. The Populists, a prairie and western reform party, the Progressives or Bull Moosers, an essentially New England reform movement, the Wilsonian Democrats with their philosophy of the New Freedom, and finally the New Deal—all questioned the old assumptions of the doctrinaire capitalist tradition. Richard Hofstader, among others, has pointed out that only the first three of these movements functioned within the framework of clearly felt moral and religious obligations of a humane nature. By conservative standards they were, accordingly, legitimate attempts to change the figures of the old tradition and substitute new figures while keeping in touch with the eternal values of Western civilization. The New Deal was a different affair altogether. It was more in the nature of improvisational emergency action without a system of underlying beliefs.

The elections of 1896 and 1900 are classic examples of the confrontation between the traditions of an old legitimate order dominated by the well-to-do Protestant upper class, whose symbol was the proper but also devout Republican William McKinley, and the claims of a new tradition, equally legitimate, carried by the rural Protestant middle and lower classes, whose champion was the flamboyant but equally devout Democrat William Jennings Bryan. How is the conservative to decide when to drop a previous symbolization in favor of a new one? A prime consideration would of course be the popularity of the new tradition. If the populace has already accepted it, conservatives must seek to advance the cause of eternal values through the new symbolization. This criterion may be applicable to the elections of 1932, 1936, 1952, or 1964, but what about the election of 1896, where there was no clear indication of the direction of public opinion? How does a conservative decide then? Probably there is no final answer to this question except Wilhelmsen's: conservatives can do no more than follow their "existential and historical preferences."

What Is American Conservatism?

The foregoing pages have served to provide a theoretical framework for an exploration of the meaning of American conservatism. Popular wisdom has it that the United States is an essentially liberal nation and, indeed, always has been throughout its history. Unfortunately, the word nation in this context is so vague as to render it unworkable. On the one hand, the American *people* have always given assent to religious and moral first principles, and while quite individualistic and forward looking, they have never allowed these feelings to distort their view of reality. At present the general populace of the nation is still surprisingly conservative, although of course the ruling powers are not. (We will return to this point at some length in Chapter 5.) However, even this liberal outlook of the American elite is a relatively recent development. In fact, until the advent of the New Deal, which from a truly rightist point of view erred not in what it did but in why it did what it did,* there was never a period in American history in which the government, the people, and the media did not proceed upon basically conservative assumptions.

The reason for the lack of understanding about the true nature of the American situation is that few social analysts of either the Right or the Left have been able to differentiate between conservatism and reaction or between reform and revolution. The French Revolution, which was a profoundly liberal revolution, has set the frame of reference for all subsequent confrontations between the "pro-reform" and "anti-reform" contingents in the Western nations. In France the changes advocated by the revolutionaries were indeed, for the most part, amoral or ideological. In America, though, the confrontations that took place between so-called liberal

*The New Deal approached society's problems from a purely materialist point of view and seemed incapable of recognizing any human needs beyond the merely economic.

108

and conservative elements before 1932 were all conducted within a framework of traditional religion, moral values, and empirical realism.* We have already advanced this thesis in regard to the McKinley-Bryan confrontations of 1896 and 1900, but it is applicable to all pre-1932 controversies of national importance.

For example: the disagreements that separated Tory loyalists from normative colonial revolutionaries (excluding, of course, Thomas Paine and his followers, who were actually leftist revolutionaries) were not as significant as is commonly supposed. Both sides appealed to the teachings of traditional faith,** classical philosophy, and objective moral values. Even the most conservative thinkers must at some point admit that when monarchy degenerates into despotism, the people must act. What is more, all rightists realize that loyalty to a sovereign means that one must overlook many of his shortcomings. In the final analysis the question is: Where does one draw the line? This is a question about which even totally committed conservatives can and do disagree.

The Federalists and the Democrats of the early years of the Republic followed the same pattern. The apologists of both groups either opposed or defended rule by "the people" on the basis of religious and objective moral considerations. Who were the liberals and conservatives in that situation? Indeed, when we reflect that nearly every American conservative thinker and politician pledges allegiance as a matter of course to almost everything the Jeffersonian and Jacksonian Democrats once advocated, it becomes clear that there was nothing unconservative about their philosophies.

The Civil War is another classic example of two factions, each emphasizing a different aspect of the conservative tradition. The South, whose agrarian, individualistic—yet aristocratic—conserv-

---

*Since America is largely a Protestant country, it possesses quite naturally the crusading and to a certain extent purist dynamism that one sees in, say, Lincoln's leadership during the Civil War or Wilson's during the First World War. This spirit, however distasteful to continental European conservatives, rarely if ever degenerated into zealotry, as the quasireligious ideological totalitarianism of the Left has done.

**The theological heresy of deism, so widespread at the time of the Revolutionary War, was a malady found among both Tories and patriots, Federalists and Antifederalists. It was not an issue that divided the various forces competing for public approval. Jefferson's religious views, for instance, were looked down upon by members of his own party as well as by his political opponents.

atism was deeply rooted in the free but devout religious spirit of that region, is often portrayed as the rightist side in that fierce struggle. Yet the North, with its defense of the nation's integral unity and its recognition that a country can ill afford to have its dissident elements simply walk out on it, was also calling upon conservative teachings about community, patriotism, and social cohesiveness to advance its position. Who was more committed to God, community, morality? Here again we must reply that both sides were equally committed. Their point of contention centered on which aspects of the same tradition should demand greater respect.

Throughout American history we witness one long continuity of metaphysically and empirically legitimate conservative positions. Superficially viewed, the rapid changes that have occurred in the two hundred years of the nation's history would seem to be a sign of leftism underlying the system. Change and reform, however, *can* be of a conservative nature. Were Moses, Christ, Maimonides, Aquinas, Francis of Assisi, and Luther conservatives or liberals? Change, if realistic—that is, nonutopian and nonideological, and committed to moral and religious first principles—is not out of step with conservatism but an important part of it. Americanism is a legitimate breed of conservatism; it rejects relativism and ideology. While its free-wheeling spirit may be somewhat atypical of Western conservatism, it is fully in keeping with Western traditions.

What is American conservatism? In its essence it is the same as any other rightism in the Western world. Its temporal symbolizations have of course varied over the years, but its basic affirmations have never changed. The forms that American conservatism assumed in the past are not our major concern in this book. Here we are primarily interested in discovering what traditions and customs of a conservative nature, true to Western values, are still viable in America today, or alternatively, if there is any popular sentiment brewing for the formulation of new traditions. This will be our express purpose in the next two chapters.

4 America 1978: Left 49, Right 0

It has long been one of the Right's weaknesses to judge its overall success or failure by gains and losses in strictly political endeavors. This failing is especially acute in America, which suffers enormously from what Jacques Ellul has termed "the political illusion"—the media-induced illusion that leads the citizenry vastly to overrate the importance of the electoral process to everyday existence. A narrow, superficial view of how societies actually function is the root cause of this popular misconception. Generally speaking, politicians merely *reflect* the mood of the country they govern. They rarely shape or deny it. Therefore, the ultimate source of the current liberal domination of the United States is not the ballot box but the academy and the media, which manipulate public opinion and influence the decisions of community leaders along leftist lines.

To rehearse in detail the changes that have taken place in America of late would require a multivolume study covering each of the various social institutions. It would be necessary to trace how scholars and academicians, together with journalists and polemicists, slowly came to reject the image of America as a moral, God-centered land providing great opportunities for the masses of men in favor of some relativist or ideological view of man and history.

111

Such a detailed study is obviously beyond the scope of this work. In the present context, however, we need not examine the rout of conservatism on every front. For our purposes it will suffice to show that the Right has been defeated in America not because its essential doctrines have been rejected by the public, but because conservatives have not related these doctrines to changing times and varying community demands with sufficient vibrancy and originality. This fact can be demonstrated by examining almost any major area of national life, for the defeatist reaction of the Right has been spread over a wide range of topics. To suit our present concern, it will be most rewarding to search out the causes of the rightist defeat in the political realm.

Before doing so, however, let us run down some of the often heard reasons for the defeat of rightists during the past two hundred years. The two reasons most commonly given for the conservative failure to halt the Left are:

1) Conservatism, because it realistically appraises man and society and advocates values that have been tested by human experience, lacks the dynamism, liveliness, and hopefulness that typify leftist thinking. It is far less appealing to say, for example, that crime has been with mankind from time immemorial and will never be eliminated, but that it can be somewhat alleviated by a reawakening of the metaphysical underpinnings of society, than it is to say that crime can be completely eliminated by funneling large sums of government aid to high-crime areas (as materialist-reductionist liberals argue), or by swiftly and severely punishing criminals (as materialist-reductionists of the Right contend).* Clearly, the true conservative position, which points to the stabilizing qualities of familial and communal cohesiveness, national purpose, and a religious orientation, is by its nature a normative and therefore somewhat unsalable item.

2) Conservatives in positions of importance in the business, political, educational, and religious worlds have all too frequently lost the will to defend their own cause. This self-imposed impotence results from either a pessimistic assessment of conservative prospects or a weakening of commitment to conservative principles. The conservative leader of any area of society is likely to come

---

*Of course, the materialist-reductionist rightist is closer to the truth than his leftist counterpart. Order must be preserved in society by punishing evildoers, but such efforts only touch the tip of the iceberg.

under the influence of men of letters who are easily disheartened by what they perceive to be the errant and isolated position of the rightist cause.

To these two themes I would like to add two more of my own:

1) Conservatives, especially the rank-and-file, tend to lack the fluidity and originality of the Left. In all probability this can be attributed to the very nature of conservatism, which emphasizes the eternal aspects of human nature as opposed to its mutable elements. As a result, conservatives are hampered by their own temperamental dispositions when they seek to rally the masses through campaign literature, rallies, media plays, or even when they seek as educators to transmit their seemingly changeless beliefs to younger generations.

2) Conservatives (and here I have in mind specifically the Right in Anglo-Saxon countries) appear to be generally quite a self-satisfied lot. They tend to evidence a certain haughtiness, a self-assuredness that puts them out of touch with the wants and needs of the majority of men. In America, too, this propensity has displayed itself: in the lack of compassion and humaneness for which liberals have often belabored the native conservative movement.

These four factors have greatly hampered the efforts of American rightists. In addition, American conservatism has suffered from a style too often crude and parochial. Over the years the public image of the American conservative has come to resemble Zenith's George Babbitt of the famous Sinclair Lewis novel. Against the trends of modernity in religion, the American Right in the early part of this century countered with a redneck affirmation of revivalist "old-time religion" rather than with a reasonable, determined, yet appealing demonstration of the basic truths of faith. The doctrinaire individualism and jingoistic imperialism that typified the Right at the turn of the century was likewise a primitive and almost childish caricature of true conservatism. To the educational theories of Deweyite relativism the Right replied with a blind defense of earlier educational methods—McGuffey readers and so on—rather than a contemporary presentation of the enduring values of a classical moral education. In sum, the natural difficulties that conservatives face in the public forum have been immensely magnified on the American scene, where rightism has for a century or more borne the stamp of either upper-class haughtiness or tub-thumping yahooism. Conservatism in America's first century, as represented by the Federalists, the National Republicans, the Whigs, and oth-

113

ers, was a noble tradition free of backwoods obscurantism. The Right of our second century, with the exception of some atypical intellectual currents, has frittered away the legacy.*

In the area of politics its consistent lack of compassion and originality has crippled the American Right. Since the last conservative president, Herbert Hoover, left Washington in March 1933, the Right has launched four nationwide campaigns for the presidency. These were the Alfred Landon campaign of 1936, the Robert Taft campaign of 1952, the Barry Goldwater campaign of 1964, and the Ronald Reagan compaign of 1976. Two of these four efforts succeeded in securing the nomination of the Republican Party, but all four eventually came up losers. By looking closely at these four conservative campaigns and the reasons why they ultimately failed, we can discern some general patterns. I have not included the three presidential campaigns of Richard Nixon and the 1976 bid of Gerald Ford on this list because, according to the political standards that conservatism has set for itself in twentieth-century America, none of these efforts could even vaguely be described as conservative, regardless of what the movement's leaders themselves had to say at the time. Whether the Nixon efforts, especially the last two, were in fact rightist according to true conservative standards is a different point altogether. Our concern at the moment is with the failure of the American Right, *as it conceived of itself,* to capture the public's fancy.

The Landon Campaign

Governor Alfred Landon of Kansas, the Republican Party standardbearer in the 1936 election, did not have the typical old-school Republican background.[1] In his youth he had supported the Bull Moosers and had, indeed, voted for Robert La Follette for president in 1924. His career in Kansas politics was marked by a long struggle against the old-guard Republican machinery of the state. When

*I have followed here the standard classification of the McKinley Right as normative conservative. According to the scheme I presented in the previous chapter, it is equally possible to view the Populists, Progressives, and some of the adherents of the New Freedom as rightists who broke out of the stereotyped image of conservatism. It should be noted, though, that the Populists were indeed ridden with redneckism and the Progressives were infected with the haughtiness of the New England reformers.

he finally overtook the frontrunners for the GOP nomination—
William Borah and Frank Knox—and the Republicans adopted a
moderate platform that, while ritually denouncing the New Deal,
grudgingly supported many of its programs, it looked as though
the traditional image of conservatism was going to be significantly
altered. This is not to say that Landon was not a true conservative
from the outset. His commitment to the underlying values of a
rural, folksy, traditionalist rightism, combined with his low-key
midwestern frankness and his apparent honesty, made him a legitimate symbol of American conservatism. He represented a fitting
alternative with which to oppose the country-squire pragmatism of
the Roosevelt administration.

The campaign began promisingly as Landon tried to convey an
image of a country-boy progressive. This was the famous "first
stage" of the campaign and it saw Landon vigorously trying to
dissociate himself from the corporate interests that controlled the
GOP hierarchy. He repudiated the support of the extreme individualists of the Liberty League and tried to keep former President
Herbert Hoover, with his bitter denunciations of the New Deal, out
of the campaign. He sought to convince national and local Republicans to include labor leaders in the campaign and to place them in
prominent positions on podiums and welcoming committees and in
parades. In late September Landon was still trying to grab the New
Deal issue away from Roosevelt as he called for drought relief, seed
loans, conservation, aid to the tenant farmer, crop insurance, and
similar programs.

There is no way to assess with total accuracy what the outcome
of the campaign would have been if Landon had stuck to his original game plan, although a comparison with the relatively successful campaign of Wendell Willkie in 1940 could shed some light on
the subject. Willkie lost, of course, but unlike Landon he came
across not as a traditionalist country boy but as the internationalist
candidate of the Eastern liberal establishment. The opportunity
that Landon had—to combine patriotic virtue with humane government—was inaccessible to Willkie. As a matter of fact, there has
never been a major-party candidate who did combine the two.

In any event, by October the Landon campaign had completely
changed its approach, in large part because of the intercession of
John Hamilton, the national chairman of the Republican Party.
Hamilton, for example, staffed the national committee's industrial
division with twenty-four workers and the labor division with only

115

three. At one point Landon even blurted out to Hamilton, "Why don't you ever bring workingmen to see me? All I ever see are stuffed-shirt businessmen and bankers."[2] As the campaign progressed, Landon went along with this new strategy of running against the New Deal. Social security, by far the most popular piece of New Deal legislation, was singled out for special treatment. In his speeches Landon constantly raised the specter of 26 million men being forced to wear dog tags inscribed with their social security numbers. Once Hamilton even held up a dog tag to reporters and claimed that the Roosevelt administration was going to compel the citizenry through social security to wear tags "such as the one I hold in my hand."[3] In a campaign speech Landon himself asked:

> Imagine the field open for federal snooping. Are these twenty-six million going to be fingerprinted? Are their photographs going to be kept on file in a Washington office? Or are they going to have identification tags around their necks?[4]

The Landon effort to portray the New Deal as some form of socialist revolution was typified by statements like that of Frank Knox, the GOP vice-presidential nominee, that "the New Deal candidate has been leading us toward Moscow."[5] Landon also questioned whether Roosevelt "intends to change the form of government."[6] Finally, in the last week of the campaign, Landon delivered what was widely heralded at the time as his most effective campaign speech at New York's Madison Square Garden. It was classic old-guard Republicanism, and as Roosevelt was to speak at the Garden only two nights later, Landon concluded his speech with a challenge to the president to answer certain questions. The contrast between the images evoked by the two addresses serves to demonstrate the severe disability of extreme laissez-faire conservatism. Landon declared:

> I come finally to the underlying and fundamental issue of the campaign. This is the question of whether our American form of government is to be preserved...
> Many of the President's actions...strike at the heart of the American form of government.
> ...life is more than bread. Character is the supreme thing. We have been weakening those very qualities upon which character is built...

116

And so in closing this meeting, I leave a challenge with the President. I say to him: Mr. President, I am willing to trust the people. I am willing to stand up and say openly that I am against economic planning by the government. I am against the concentration of power...

Tell us where you stand, Mr. President. Tell us not in generalities, but clearly, so that no one can mistake your meaning...[7]

Two nights later Roosevelt stood on the same podium and replied to Landon:

Tonight I call the roll—the roll of honor of those who stood with us in 1932 and still stand with us today.

Written on it are the names of millions who never had a chance—men at starvation wages, women in sweatshops, children at looms...

For twelve years this nation was afflicted with hear-nothing, see-nothing, do-nothing government. The nation looked to government but the government looked away. Nine mocking years with the Golden Calf and three long years of the scourge. Nine crazy years at the ticker and three long years in the breadlines! Nine mad years of mirage and three long years of despair! Powerful influences strive today to restore that kind of government with its doctrine that that government is best which is most indifferent...

[In] my first Administration [these] forces of selfishness met their match!...

This is our answer to those who, silent about their own plans, ask us to state our objectives.

Of course we will continue to improve working conditions for the workers of America...*Of course* we will continue to work for cheaper electricity in the homes and on the farms of America...*Of course* we will continue our efforts for young men and women...for the crippled, for the blind, for the mothers, our insurance for the unemployed, our security for the aged...

For these things...and for a multitude of things like them, we have only begun to fight.[8]

Here we see the difference between the styles of the American Right and Left. The average citizen, when confronted with these two statements, is left with the obvious impression that conserva-

117

tives are somber prophets calling for a return to Puritan virtues, insensitive to the yearnings and wants of the average citizen. The Landon effort, by refusing to flatter the voters and appeal to them *on their own terms,* was repeating the old mistakes of the American Right that had doomed John Adams to defeat in 1800 and John Quincy Adams in 1828. The American conservative has never been able to understand this obvious and elemental fact of democratic politics. *Ancien régime* kings and the nationalist leaders of the post–World War I European Right were successful because they won the respect and love of the citizenry by creating a plausible impression of themselves as friends of the common man. (In truth, of course, this impression was more mythopoetic imagery than mundane reality.) The Russian common man, for example, almost always viewed the czar as his compassionate Holy Father and St. Petersburg as the place of redress for his grievances. One of the most common themes in Russian folklore is that of the peasant or serf who, having gotten a bad deal from some lord or other adversary, finally manages by some fantastic means to present his case to the czar, who invariably sides with him in his problem. This imagery was, to be sure, fanciful. The fact is that there were good czars and bad czars, moral czars and corrupt czars, and so on. But the key factor in maintaining the stability of the community and the satisfaction of the citizenry was the favorable image of czardom as an institution to which the people could show allegiance through its living head.

Now, in a democracy the maintaining of images is a much more difficult job. The politician is constantly called upon to bare his soul, his personality, and every nuance of his views to the public. To succeed, a politician must learn to relate to the often clumsily expressed needs and aspirations of the population. Franklin Delano Roosevelt was a classic example of how to master the methods of the mass-suffrage process. Conservatives, on the other hand, since the days of the Federalists, have spoken above or around the people, rather than *to* them, and have payed little attention to the effects of their actions. As early as 1801, perceptive conservatives seem to have sensed that playing in the democratic ball park calls for slightly different strategy. On January 26 of that year, in the aftermath of the Jefferson presidential victory, Fisher Ames wrote to John Rutledge Jr., another old-school Federalist, "We must court popular favor. We must study public opinion and accommodate measures to what it is."[9]

118

Unfortunately, Landon did not follow Ames' advice, and the result was that he failed as had John and John Quincy Adams before him. His presidential bid was the most decisively defeated of any until that time. Why? Basically, because Landon gave his allegiance (at least during the crucial months of the campaign) to the outdated forms of a once dominant conservative order. The Landon defeat was a crucial turning point in American history. It resulted in the elimination of the old-guard conservatives from positions of importance in the GOP for a twenty-eight-year period during which the Eastern liberal wing of the party dictated policy and picked its own candidates. These candidates were not compassionate religious men in the William Jennings Bryan mold, but materialist-reductionists or, as we now call them, secular humanists. The Republican Party was thus forced to come to a twenty-eight-year peace with the welfare state, conservatism was discredited in America, and Roosevelt and Truman were the leaders of our country in the tragic early years of the Cold War. Could Landon have won if he had stuck to his early campaign intentions? It is unlikely. Roosevelt had everything going for him that year. But even if Landon had not won, a closer election would have significantly altered the ensuing years for the Right. The Republican Party could have remained in conservative hands and the Right could have been a force to be reckoned with in American politics. In fact, however, the conservatives were utterly defeated. Retiring to their old haunts, they virtually disappeared as a force in American life.

The Taft Campaign

Senator Robert A. Taft of Ohio was the political leader of the American Right during some of its darkest days. From the beginning of the New Deal and his famous 1935 lawsuit against the Treasury Department to compel it to honor the gold backing of pre-1933 money until his final defeat at the Republican convention in 1952, he was, without a doubt, Mr. Conservative in the public mind. Taft was given to violent denunciations of the New Deal. In fact, this was probably the central reason for his great popularity among conservatives. In 1933 he predicted that the New Deal, if left intact, would cause us "to abandon the whole theory of American government, and inaugurate what is in fact socialism."[10] Beyond his old-guard conservative opinions, though, the Ohioan possessed an honesty and personal integrity that were widely admired by all who knew him. Taft was a rare bird among politicians, whose ambitions generally ride roughshod over their ideals (when they have any). He firmly believed in the principles he expressed and innumerable times throughout his career he sacrificed personal advantage in order to defend them. When anti-German feeling ran high at the time of the Nuremberg trials, Taft opposed the whole idea of trying the Nazi leaders as war criminals. This position, which brought upon him a firestorm of personal abuse, was typical of the integrity of this courageous man.

Apparently, though, God seldom taps exceptionally virtuous politicians for high national office. Taft's high moral character was his undoing. He spoke his mind and he did so with a seriousness that was proper for the topics he dealt with. He was not a crowd pleaser and, except for a brief period late in his career, did not seek to be one. When he felt that the New Deal would lead to "the destruction of our system and probably a socialistic state," he said so. [11] When he felt that "if Roosevelt is not a Communist today, he is bound to become one," he said so. [12] When asked what could be done to alleviate the effects of rising food costs, he briskly replied, "Eat less." [13] Besides these doctrinal impediments, Taft also suffered from the personality characteristics that had come to be connected with McKinley-Hoover Republicanism. He disdained to show emotion in public and came across to those who did not know him as a cold man lacking compassion.

All of these drawbacks were ironically unfortunate for the American Right. Of the four presidential candidates the Right has fielded in the past forty years, Taft was the only one who was clearly *not* a doctrinaire antistatist. Landon was perhaps unsure of his ideals. But Goldwater, whom we will soon examine, was an ardent exponent of laissez-faire, while Reagan, after a rough bout with the welfare state in the New Hampshire primary, basically ignored the economic issue. Taft, on the other hand, was the closest thing to an American Disraeli that the conservative movement has produced in contemporary times. Despite his strong-sounding rhetoric, he actually favored federal aid in a wide variety of areas. He supported public housing, minimum wage laws, increased social security benefits, federal aid to education, and grants to hospitals. In addition, Taft in his private life sympathized with and was greatly troubled by the plight of the unfortunate. But he was unable to convey the essence of his rightism to the people. In the aftermath of the 1936 Roosevelt victory over Landon, Taft attributed the result to the Democrat's ability to appear as a "friend of the poor man and against the rich man."[14] Toward the end of his career, during the 1950 Senate race, Taft hired a public relations firm to help improve his image with the voters. So the Ohioan was aware of the difficulties in selling old-school conservatism to the people, but he was unable to extricate himself from those very problems.

In Taft American conservatism had a supreme opportunity to strike out in a new direction. The potentialities, however, stand in stark contrast to the realities of the 1952 Republican primary campaign—Taft's last attempt to wrest control of the party from its Eastern liberal wing.[15] On October 16, 1951 Taft announced his candidacy and pledged himself to wage a vigorous campaign for "liberty rather than the principles of socialism."[16] From the outset the senator, although acknowledged as the frontrunner in the race, had problems winning popular support. The polls bore this out. Gallup, for example, consistently showed General Eisenhower, at that time an undeclared candidate, easily capable of beating either Truman, Stevenson, or Kefauver, but showed that Taft could barely beat Truman and would lose overwhelmingly to Stevenson or Kefauver.[17] These factors encouraged the Republican liberals to seek to persuade the General to return home from Europe and abandon his position as Supreme Commander of NATO in order to oppose Taft in the primaries. Eisenhower refused, but despite his "phantom candidacy," as the Taft people called it, he handed Taft a sound defeat in the New Hampshire primary on March 11, 1952. This set the stage for the difficult primary campaign between Taft and Eisenhower, with Eisenhower eventually coming home to campaign in person and ultimately defeating Taft at one of the bitterest Republican conventions ever held.

Most students of that convention have concluded that although the majority of the delegates personally favored Taft, they felt that the Ohioan's individualism and neo-isolationism were liabilities that he could not overcome in a national campaign. The *New York Times*, always first in reader services, published a three-part editorial in June entitled "Mr. Taft Can't Win."[18] Worse, the *Times* was proved true by all the major polls, which invariably depicted Taft as the underdog against any Democratic candidate. Upon losing the nomination Taft attributed his loss to lack of time to make an adequate campaign against newspaper influence.[19] He failed to realize that the newspapers got away with what they did because of the nature of his candidacy. Roosevelt battled for years against the major newspapers and beat them at their own game. He went over their heads and appealed directly to the people. If Taft had done the same, if he could have changed his public image, then the popular impression of his electoral inability could perhaps have been overcome. The Taft campaign was a singular opportunity for twentieth-century American conservatism to relate to the American people. It passed and nothing similar has as yet come along.

In the aftermath of the Taft defeat a large segment of the American Right began to develop a mythology—and mythology is the only possible word for it—that the American people were overwhelmingly conservative and that those millions of Americans who traditionally stay at home on election day were all die-hard rightists disenchanted by "me-too" Republican candidates. This view, as absurd as it may seem today, was widely held in conservative circles and was popularized over the years by works such as Clarence Manion's *The Conservative American* and Ralph de Toledano's *The Winning Side.* Rightists came to believe that Taft had been robbed of the nomination. Had he been the candidate, he would have won. Conservatives felt that all that was needed to score a decisive rightist victory at the polls would be to put up a candidate preaching laissez-faire and strict constitutional construction. The clear evidence of 1932, 1936, and the Taft primary effort, and the unanimous testimony of the pollsters—all of which showed that a huge majority of Americans supported the basic concepts of the New Deal—were ignored. Through the fifties and early sixties American conservatives bided their time, waiting for the day when the millions of rugged individualists would all emerge from their hiding places because the Republican Party was finally offering "a choice, not an echo."

The Goldwater Campaign

In 1964 the old guard of the American Right got its chance. The conservative wing of the Republican Party finally had its way and Senator Barry Goldwater received the presidential nomination. Here at last, rightists believed, was the man who could get the nonvoting conservative majority to the polls. Goldwater had inherited Taft's title of Mr. Conservative and he certainly deserved it. The Arizonan stood without compromise for everything old-guard conservatism had stood for. He dismissed all federal involvement in the fields of education, agriculture, welfare, and foreign aid as unconstitutional and unwise. His devotion to strict construction and market economics was just about as pure as could be imagined and his foreign-policy proposals we have already examined at some length in Chapter 1. To boot, Goldwater fired the emotions of American rightists as neither Hoover, Landon, Taft, Bricker, MacArthur, nor other favorites had ever been capable of doing. This was due in no small measure to Goldwater's friendly, rustic, and lively personality. Goldwater broke the media stereotype of conservatives as either somber (Taft), haughty (MacArthur), or vicious (Joseph McCarthy). Goldwater's affable, let-your-hair-down attitude appealed to friend and foe alike. After all, who could fail to like a man who, when he saw reporters staring at his obviously book-filled suitcase, smiled broadly and said, "Don't worry, fellas, it's all full of Mickey Spillane. That's all."[20] In Goldwater the Right finally had a candidate that articulated its case without reservation and projected an appealing personality. For conservatives, 1964 seemed to be the year when the "revolution of 1932" could finally be reversed.

In point of fact, 1964 was in all probability the year in which the question of the government's entry into the social-welfare field was settled forever. Goldwater was defeated by a landslide unprecedented in American history. In the ensuing fourteen years conservatives have been offering all sorts of excuses for the Goldwater debacle. They have pointed to the Kennedy assassination, to Johnson's Southern appeal, to the influence of the media, to the ousting of the F. Clifton White group of campaign strategists in favor of the "Arizona mafia," to the poor behavior of the Goldwater people at the convention during the Rockefeller antiextremism speech, to the unwise vice-presidential choice, and a host of other factors. In sum, rightists have refused to believe what all the polls of that election year revealed: that the American people were simply scared out of their wits by Goldwater's proposals to dismantle the welfare state and take the Cold War to the Communists, and his seeming opposition to civil rights. A Louis Harris poll taken shortly before the election showed that the voters considered Goldwater a "radical" who would seriously weaken long-accepted government economic programs.[21] The voters saw Goldwater as opposed to medicare and the antipoverty program, which 69 percent favored; they believed that he wanted to sell TVA, a move they opposed by a two-to-one

123

margin.[22] Gallup polls throughout 1964 also consistently showed that the voters favored a candidate who would be "for civil rights" —and they didn't mean Goldwater.[23] During the campaign, Harris polls showed that between 48 and 65 percent of the American people feared that Goldwater would "weaken" the social security system,[24] which was supported by nine out of ten Americans at its inception and has consistently been the favorite federal welfare program of the citizenry.

Most of all, though, it was Goldwater's use of the swashbuckling liberation rhetoric of fifties conservatism that frightened the electorate. More than seven out of ten voters just two weeks before the 1964 election believed that Goldwater as president would "start a war with Cuba."[25] Fifty-eight percent feared he would drop atomic bombs on North Vietnam.[26] Seventy percent were convinced that Goldwater as president would "act before thinking."[27] The Harris poll revealed on October 19, 1964 that over half of those planning to vote for Johnson intended to do so because they were afraid Goldwater's election would lead to war.[28] The important fact to bear in mind here is that these popular impressions were not the result of media distortions, but were on the whole accurate. Goldwater did oppose medicare and the antipoverty program. On social security his record was contradictory; at times he had completely opposed it, at other times he wanted to make it voluntary, and when the campaign got serious he suddenly wanted to strengthen it. Goldwater did want to repeal most of the New Deal–Fair Deal legislation. On foreign policy he had advocated a Cuban invasion and had talked loosely about using atomic weapons in Asia. Were those fears of war groundless? Goldwater had repeatedly advanced the thesis that it was far better to "run the risk of war" in order to "destroy the Soviet empire" than to seek merely to coexist with and contain Communism. The American people did not misread Mr. Conservative. They read him quite accurately and rejected him decisively.

American conservatives have been selling each other almost as many myths about what happened in 1964 as they once sold each other about what was going to happen in 1964. For example, we are told that the media falsely sought to portray Goldwater as unpopular among the Republican rank-and-file. "Not so," say conservatives. "He received the largest popular vote in the primaries." What conservative polemicists neglect to add is that Goldwater's primary-vote total was vastly inflated by the inclusion of states like

Illinois, Nebraska, Texas, and others where the senator ran virtually unopposed. (Harold Stassen or Margaret Chase Smith was the typical opposition.) All the polls showed that Goldwater's popularity among Republicans steadily declined throughout the primary campaign. Gallup showed that the Arizonan, although never a favorite of the GOP voters, actually lost nearly half his following from December 1963, when 27 percent of the Republicans were behind him, to April 1964, when only 14 percent still wanted Goldwater to be the nominee.[29] In late June, when Governor William Scranton of Pennsylvania launched a last-minute campaign to stop Goldwater, Scranton—a relative unknown—swung the majority of Republicans behind him. A Gallup poll taken on June 28, just two weeks before the convention where Goldwater was to receive the huge majority of delegate votes, revealed that 55 percent of the Republican rank-and-file favored Scranton, with only 34 percent backing Goldwater and 11 percent undecided.[30] Yet conservatives have been ignoring the evidence on these matters. There is little doubt that the American people devastatingly rejected Goldwater not because of his personality, which they found affable, but because of his opinions, which they viewed as extreme and threatening.

The Goldwater campaign represented both the high point and the end of the revival of McKinley-Hoover rightism that began in the fifties. For a few fleeting weeks between Goldwater's victory over Rockefeller in the California primary and the moment when J. Drake Evans, chairman of the South Carolina delegation, announcing that his state was "humbly grateful that it can do this for America," put the Arizonan over the top at the Republican convention, the American Right lived in a state of euphoria. During that brief period conservatives convinced themselves that they had indeed triumphed—that this was it—and that with their books and periodicals they had actually convinced the American people to return to the Tenth Amendment and William Graham Sumner.

Sad to say, it was not long before the sobering realities of popular sentiment put an end to the heady dreams that had electrified the San Francisco Cow Palace. From the beginning of the campaign Goldwater was the underdog. He was forced to go on the defensive. With the polls showing him a consistent two-to-one loser, the old conservative theory that millions of closet rightists were waiting to vote for a candidate who would annihilate the Communists and restore laissez-faire looked pretty incredible. As the weeks dragged

125

on, the Goldwater campaign became little more than an extended effort to play down the Arizonan's hard-line conservatism. Republican literature went to great lengths to emphasize that Goldwater did not, in fact, want to make social security voluntary, sell TVA, overturn *Brown*, or eliminate price supports for farmers. One Goldwater campaign pamphlet, featuring the senator with his children and grandchildren, was entitled "Ten Reasons Why Barry Goldwater Wants Peace." The only way the Goldwater team thought it had a chance of victory was by denying those principles of fifties conservatism which the senator and his followers had always held to be basic and nonnegotiable.

As the final returns proved, even this diluted version of Goldwaterism was unpalatable to the overwhelming majority of Americans. Mr. Conservative of 1964 was rejected by some sixty percent of the nation and managed to carry but six states (including Alabama, where he ran unopposed). After this crushing defeat the American Right seemed to stop taking itself and its programs very seriously. Although bumper stickers now proclaimed "26 Million Americans Can't Be Wrong," conservatives had in truth abandoned all hope of enforcing the Tenth Amendment, dismantling the welfare state, or destroying international Communism. The story of American conservatism since 1964 has been that of a movement in search of a philosophy. American conservatism has been looking for a reason to exist.

The Reagan Campaign

There was much talk among conservatives after the disgrace of the Nixon administration about the need to forge the New Majority of which we have previously spoken. This rightist coalition was supposed to unite Americans who, unlike the liberal intelligentsia, were still dedicated to traditional beliefs, values, and lifestyles. Various proposals were put forward: to form a third party headed by George Wallace or Ronald Reagan, or alternatively, to support both of these men in their respective parties and hope to unite the coalition later. It seemed at the time that rightists were beginning to reevaluate the image they projected and were seriously interested in broadening their ranks beyond those determined 26 million of 1964.

When Ronald Reagan announced his candidacy on November

20, 1975, it appeared that rightists were willing to acclimate themselves to the realities of twentieth-century politics. In Reagan they had a charismatic figure who, though still not radiating the same fiery identification with "the people" as Franklin D. Roosevelt or Robert F. Kennedy, was beyond a doubt the most personally attractive individual of the four conservatives mentioned here. Despite these points in his favor a problem remained: how to translate Reagan's well-to-do Far Western image into one with which urban ethnics, rural midwesterners, and traditionalist-leaning citizens generally could identify—people who have little in common with what Frederick Wilhelmsen refers to as "dough conservatives."

Unfortunately, all the questions about how to portray Reagan in New Majority images were academic, for the Reagan campaign from the opening of the race sought to embrace the symbols of a long-since-outdated conservatism. In the New Hampshire primary, the first of the campaign, Reagan offered a proposal to return $90 billion worth of federal aid programs back to the individual states to administer them. Now, the relative merits of this proposal are not germane to the present discussion. The important fact is that Reagan, after all the talk about New Majority politics, decided to launch his campaign with a proposal that conjured up all the familiar memories of harsh old-school conservatism. Image is the key word here, for if Reagan had gone into New Hampshire and delivered several talks about, say, the plight of the unemployed and the need for some version of the Kemp bill, or the crippling costs of hospitalization and the need to alleviate the plight of the middle class in this area, garnishing his speeches with compassionate, understanding phrases, then—and only then, after neutralizing the media—could he have gone on to the $90 billion plan. As it was, the proposal became a millstone around Reagan's neck. Amazingly, his high command resolved to defend it at all costs. Throughout the New Hampshire and the Florida primaries Reagan continued to advocate this plan despite the obvious fact that it was costing him popular support and exposing him to ridicule in the media. The slim margins by which the Californian was defeated in both states could very possibly have been reversed but for the $90 billion blunder.

Finally, after a string of primary losses that were ultimately fatal to his campaign, Reagan changed two features of his strategy. First, he took the offensive in violation of his self-proclaimed "eleventh commandment" not to speak ill of any other Republican.

He became strongly critical of the Ford administration. Second, although he continued the standard catch-phrase Republican rhetoric of balanced budgets and individual freedom, he dropped his criticism of government intervention in the economy. In the aftermath of the North Carolina primary, which was Reagan's first victory and was widely credited with turning his campaign around, the polls showed that the decisive factor in the balloting had been a statewide half-hour television piece in which Reagan attacked the Ford-Kissinger foreign policy.[31] Foreign policy was also the key to the massive Reagan victory over Ford in Texas, which boosted his stock enormously. Whereas old-school antistatism hurt Reagan, the foreign-policy issue strengthened him.

It is, of course, difficult to generalize about politics. Even if Reagan had won the nomination, it would have been an uphill battle for him all the way. He would have had to face the inevitable propagandistic shelling from the media. Of this much, however, we can be fairly certain: had Reagan not broached the $90 billion scheme in New Hampshire or criticized the TVA in Tennessee, in short, if he had left the economic status quo undisturbed (or better still, if he had attempted to be what Taft could have been, an American Disraeli, a traditionalist friend of the common man), he could have deflected the hostility of the media. Reagan's failure was all too typical of the post-1932 American Right.

Conclusion

Thus we end our brief review of conservative political endeavors in post-1932 America. We have concentrated on four campaigns for the presidency, but the same conclusions could be drawn from hundreds of congressional campaigns. Two themes predominate. First, the American conservative movement has failed to understand and relate to the aspirations of the majority of men. Second, the American Right has clung to an imagery that may have been appealing in the 1890s, but frightens the contemporary citizenry. These are the practical considerations. On a deeper level, American conservatism has forgotten what it was trying to conserve. The Right is surely devoted to the preservation of a great deal more than the pre-World War I economic order. But American conservatism fails to see this, having been to a large extent cut off from its roots in the Western tradition. It is enlightening in this connection to note that Russell Kirk in his celebrated work *The Conservative Mind,* which traces the development of American and English conservatism, does not include so much as one thinker genuinely representative of the Right in America's second century. Instead, he bemoans the extreme individualism of the era while ignoring the fact that this very individualism was a rightist, not a leftist phenomenon. Kirk chooses to dwell on such atypical conservatives of the period as Brooks and Henry Adams, and Irving Babbitt and Paul Elmer More. These men, however, were certainly not in the conservative mainstream of their day, nor were they part of the conservative revival of the fifties.

Beginning with the Gilded Age, the American Right came to view itself in a grossly distorted manner. Except for isolated individuals, it no longer thought of itself as one with the Federalists, Whigs, or National Republicans, or even with the Antifederalist Southern agrarian Democrats, but as part of a utopian evolutionary process (survival of the fittest and manifest destiny were the buzz words) whereby Americans would democratize and capitalize the world. The capitalist-jingoist mentality that gave us the Spanish-American War and World War I (in which America destroyed the Habsburg monarchy—the backbone of a faltering European civilization) resulted from this Babbitt-style old-conservative spirit. It *was* a conservative spirit. But it was warped.

When this boisterous conservatism died in the Depression, the American Right was duty bound to search its conscience. It did not. Landon, Taft, Goldwater, and Reagan were all symbols—with different nuances, to be sure—of late nineteenth-century conservatism. Goldwater was perhaps the closest imitation of the big-stick-carrying jingoist and doctrinaire libertarian. Of the four he was the most soundly rejected by the American people. Looking over this history of defeat, one is reminded of the reply of Maryland Senator Millard Tydings, Sr., a virulent opponent of the New Deal, when asked what the prospects were for his conservatism. He answered, "There are none. I have simply outlived my time."

Must conservatives therefore conclude that the battle is lost? Is American conservatism a doomed persuasion, making a last stand at the Alamo against the forces of modernity? Is there any hope of reviving conservatism in contemporary America? This will be the subject of the following chapter.

5 Can a Street Corner Wear a Sun Belt?

It has long been the position of rightist thinkers that the great mass of men in any normative society are conservative. That is, their primary concerns are those which the Right has always shared. The average citizen is interested in family cohesiveness and material security. He longs for a sense of some higher purpose in life, and a feeling of his significance as an individual. Most people pursue these seemingly modest goals within a religious and moral framework that they absorb from their parents, relatives, schools, and communities. To the rightist, a society functions well if it satisfies these inherent needs of the populace by supporting the family and relieving material and spiritual distress. A healthy society, for him, emphasizes the patriotic-communal and religious-moral aspects of life.

Measured by these standards, despite what some conservative theoreticians might say to the contrary, the American people have been and are conservative. The governing educational and media elite of the nation may have opted in this century for the heresies of amoralism or ideology, but the citizenry simply has not. (Indeed, whether the masses in any society ever really do is questionable.) This split between the people and the pacesetters of society is a relatively recent development. Until the first quarter of the twen-

130

tieth century the public appearance of America was basically representative of the feelings of its people. Even the disagreements that have raged in our country in the past were fought out in a conservative setting. Both Federalists and Antifederalists, Democrats and Whigs, appealed to classical philosophy, revealed religion, and patriotic loyalty, as did both the North and the South during the Civil War era.* In addition, as I have stated before, the controversies between Protestant Republican old-school libertarians and the Democratic reformers and later the Bull Moose Progressives were all conducted within a traditionalist framework. Wilsonism, although its foreign policy was tinged with intolerant utopianism, was a sincerely moral, conservative force, as Russell Kirk among others has shown. Of course, not all conservative symbolizations of one era can excite rightists of other times, but the point to remember is that they were relevant to the years in which they flourished. Taken as a group these movements all reflect assorted moods of American traditionalism.**

There is a certain optimism in the American mind, an emphasis on progress and breaking with the past that at first appears to be the very opposite of conservative. I cannot stress sufficiently, however, that these themes are for all practical purposes American *myths*. The people of this country have never let their optimism overstep the bounds of legitimacy and lead them to the natural

---

*The "age of Jackson" was a bit below par next to these other traditions, but the followers of Old Hickory were another legitimate manifestation of American populism. They exhibited the same loyalty to God, family, country, and community common to this American phenomenon. They were crude, perhaps, but conservative.

**I am well aware that for the Catholic or Jewish rightist, American conservative symbols leave something to be desired. They carry heavy Protestant overtones. The pure-faith crusading spirit of, say, Lincoln Republicanism or Bull Moose Progressivism is not the sort of thing with which Catholics or Jews can easily sympathize. However, the task of conservatives is to improve the temporal order in a realistic manner, not to damage their own interests by dreaming idle dreams. Moreover, one is tempted to ask European Catholic conservatives whether they feel completely at ease with the neopaganism of certain elements of French and especially Italian and German rightism, for whom the disastrous turning point in Western history was not the French Revolution but the rejection of Roman and Nordic paganism in favor of Christianity. Surely Catholic conservatives would agree that the democrats of 1828 or 1896 more faithfully embodied the essence of conservatism than did the *Squadristi* or the S.S.!

corollary of leftist optimism, which is utopian totalitarianism. Nor has their belief in progress led them to abandon traditional values. That they have never broken radically with the past is confirmed by their widespread adherence, even today, to orthodox religious faith.

The tenor of public life was cut off from the mood of the general populace sometime early in the twentieth century, as the Left, for many reasons, some of which we have gone into before, gained control of the country's political, educational, and communications establishment. The result is that society's leaders today have distinctly different views about God, family, country, and morality from those of the people they supposedly lead. The American people as a whole are patriotic in the old-fashioned sense of the term; they believe in the God of traditional faith; they reject the "new morality"; they want the country to adopt a strong and prestigious foreign policy. At the same time, the liberal elite ridicules all these positions.

Why, then, have American conservatives failed to capitalize on these circumstances? By now the answer should be quite obvious: the rightist attachment to laissez-faire and belligerent foreign-policy rhetoric has become unpalatable to the average contemporary American. This defeat by default, so to speak, was tragic. For while American conservatives severed the links that have normally joined the Right with the man in the street, this same man in the street was looking for an ally to help him fight the elitist domination of his schools, media, and government. The fault here has not been the citizen's. Who could blame him for not accepting men like Hoover, Taft, or Goldwater as his allies? They never understood his concerns in the first place.

The Humane People

It is not especially difficult to substantiate this line of argument. The American people like to think of themselves as decent and compassionate. That the widespread suffering of the Great Depression caused them to endorse the basic assumptions of the New Deal should have come as no surprise. Disregarding guaranteed national income plans from Huey Long's to George McGovern's, the Gallup polls reveal that with only *four exceptions* over a thirty-six-year period (1935–1971) the American people have never opposed

132

any government program to help those in need.* In fact, three of those four exceptional polls involved programs of questionable constitutionality. (Or so the courts of that era felt; two were on the NRA and one was on the AAA).[1] The constitutional factor could easily have influenced the public in those cases. To cite some random examples from the thirties, eight out of ten Americans favored an amendment to the Constitution prohibiting child labor (Gallup, March 28, 1936); six out of ten wanted minimum wage laws (Gallup, June 6, 1937); nine out of ten supported social security (Gallup, January 12, 1936); seven out of ten favored federal aid to education (Gallup, March 26, 1938); eight out of ten wanted the federal government to "provide free medical aid for those unable to pay" (Gallup, June 14, 1937); seven out of ten claimed that "it is the government's responsibility to pay the living expenses of those who are out of work" (Gallup, April 5, 1939), while three-quarters of the people felt that "the government should see to it that any man who wants to work has a job."[2] These feelings have continued down to our own day, with large majorities of Americans supporting an increase in the minimum wage (Gallup, September 29, 1965), low-interest federal housing loans (Harris, *Newsweek,* January 11, 1965), the antipoverty program and medicare (Harris, *Newsweek,* October 19, 1964), the Community Action and Head Start programs,[3] and so on. Even during the supposedly conservative Nixon administration a poll revealed that 64 percent of the American people favored a "proposal that the federal government guarantee a job to every American who wants to work even if it means creating a lot of public jobs like during the Depression."[4]

While consistently and overwhelmingly supporting welfarism, the American public remains equally committed to the idea of a balanced budget. Americans also like the idea of taking power away from Washington. This amazing contradiction has been noted in *The Political Beliefs of Americans,*[5] where authors Lloyd Free and Hardy Cantril explain it by differentiating between the "operational" and "ideological" beliefs of Americans. By "ideological" beliefs the authors mean the mythical identification that the American people still have with the symbols of an earlier era, such as balanced budgets and states' rights, while by "operational" beliefs they refer to the *real* beliefs of the citizenry—the

*Over a hundred polls showed majority support for various aid programs.

133

positions that people take on a day-to-day basis, namely, favoring government aid programs.

Free and Cantril have logically solved the problem, but in fairness one more factor should be mentioned. The man in the street is not very well versed in the intricacies of domestic or foreign problems. As the polls have repeatedly shown, his ignorance of even the most fundamental matters is, to say the least, startling. How, then, does he arrive at his opinions on such complicated issues as medicare or the balanced budget? The answer, I believe, is that his positions are the result of what we may describe as the "nice-guy" syndrome. He will invariably opt for whatever answer appears "nice" in the context. Thus, a question like "Should we be firm with the Communists?" will always be answered in the affirmative because "firm" is a nice word in that context. However, a question like "Should we negotiate with the Communists for peace?" will also be answered yes because "negotiate" and "peace" are the nice words. Similarly, on economic issues, if the question is something like "Should we have a system to help those citizens unable to pay their own medical expenses?" the answer will always be yes, but a question like "Should the federal budget be balanced during the next fiscal year?" will also be answered yes because both helping the needy and balancing budgets are nice things to do. It is impossible to understand public opinion polls without coming to this conclusion. What is important for our purposes, though, is that when push comes to shove and the American people must choose between laissez-faire states' rights candidates who will *really* attempt to balance the budget and others who affirm the government's obligation to assist the citizenry in their satisfaction of basic needs while rendering mythical homage to balanced budgets, they vote "operationally" and not "ideologically"—by an overwhelming margin.

The American people are not, of course, socialists. The polls testify to their steady opposition, even in the heady early New Deal days, to any measures for redistribution of wealth or property, or state ownership of the means of production. Additionally, the polls confirm the common impression that Americans are great respecters of hard work, self-sacrifice, diligence, and the like. The only lasting result of the Great Depression and the New Deal was that people came to demand that government help those who, because of circumstances beyond their control, *cannot help themselves.* Herein lies the significance of the public furore over welfare fraud, in which old-guard conservatives take so much encouragement.

The people resent the fact that it is all too easy for the undeserving individual to get on the welfare rolls. When the public clamors about high welfare costs, it is not professing loyalty to either the Chicago or the Austrian school of laissez-faire economics. The ordinary American believes that there *is* such a thing as a free lunch and that it should be given to those who are unable to buy one, but not, of course, to those who *are* able.

On the other hand, Americans continue to be seriously concerned about rising taxes. Obviously, one cannot have the matter both ways. The current federal budget must inevitably result in high taxes for the citizenry. The solution to this dilemma? Probably something along the lines of Governor Reagan's systematic welfare reform in California, under which numerous ineligibles were dropped from state aid programs while payments to the truly needy were increased. However, the key point here, as we have remarked before, is the image that the Right conveys. Emphasis must be laid upon the humane aspects of the program. Conservatives must demonstrate effectively that they are just as concerned as the Left about the destitute, the aged, the sick, and the crippled. They, not the Left, must traverse the big-city slums, Appalachian country roads, and blue-collar factories when they campaign. In a word, conservatives must care about the things the majority of the country cares about, and must show it. Rightists would do well to heed the sage counsel of that early American conservative, Alexander Hamilton, who wrote during the decline of the old Federalist party in April of 1802:

> We must consider whether it is possible for us to succeed, without in some degree employing the weapons which have been employed against us.[6]

The Virtuous People

To my mind, one of the most surprising themes that emerge from the study of contemporary American opinion is the degree to which our people have remained loyal to the basic principles of traditional faith and moral values despite the relativist onslaught of the elitist elements in society during the last fifty years or so. Ninety-eight percent of Americans believe in God.[7] Sixty-three percent of the citizenry prays frequently,[8] and church attendance for the sects least affected by the forces of secularism—the Baptists, Lutherans, and other evangelical groups—has risen in recent years. The more "moderate" groups like the Presbyterians and the Episcopalians have held a fairly constant percentage of worshipers. All the well-publicized statistics about the decline in church attendance are attributable to two faiths, Catholicism and Judaism. Yet the drop in Catholic attendance only began in the period of liberalism following Vatican II. And Catholic traditionalists, who remain firmly attached to their faith, have actually shown some signs of growth with new periodicals, schools, and seminaries. Similarly, if we eliminate from the figures on Jewish worship those of the Reform and Conservative groups, as well as the elderly Orthodox Jews who came to America during the 1881–1923 period when Sabbath observance was extremely difficult and whose children therefore drifted away from their faith, we find that Orthodox Judaism is rapidly growing and its synagogue-attendance figures are up over earlier years.

On moral issues the American people are traditionalist without being prudish. They feel overwhelmingly (80 percent) that "morality in the country is declining."[9] Over 75 percent would like to see "stricter laws on the sale of pornography."[10] (Apparently, about 5 percent of Americans are both traditionalist and libertarian: 80 percent of the citizenry finds pornography "*personally* objectionable.")[11] Supposedly outdated sexual ethics are also supported by the people, for over 65 percent oppose any kind of premarital sex, even among couples engaged to be married.[12] Some 70 percent of the population does not want to encourage promiscuity by making birth control pills available to high school and college students.[13] Divorce laws should also be made "stricter" according to the majority.[14] Just the same, Americans do not feel that young people should be kept ignorant of the facts of sex; only that they should order their lives in accordance with the dictates of Judeo-Christian morality. They do support sex education in the schools.[15] This is not, however, a recent development. Long before the elitists endorsed the "new morality," the man in the street supported sex education. Whether he was wise to do so is of course a different matter altogether,* but his position should not be miscontrued as acceptance of the amoralism of the elite.

---

*Probably the public is ignorant of the fact that most sex education programs operate outside of any value framework and can only create in the student's mind a disposition in favor of moral relativism.

In the area of crime and punishment Americans are equally conservative. Over 75 percent of the people feel that criminals are not treated strictly enough in this country, while those favoring conservative appointees to the Supreme Court outnumbered those favoring liberal ones by an almost two-to-one margin.[16] In every Gallup poll taken since 1935, with the exception of one, the majority of Americans have endorsed capital punishment. At the height of the student disorders of the sixties, 94 percent of the American people wanted "to see college administrators take a stronger stand."[17] In fact, during the demonstrations at the 1968 Democratic convention the public refused to accept the media's portrayal of the events and by a 56 to 21 percent margin felt that the police were not "using excessive force in suppressing" the demonstrators.[18] Later, over 70 percent of the public, in direct contradiction to the media image, opined that the Chicago Seven received a fair trial from Judge Hoffman.[19] On the issue of marijuana, which is symbolic of the assault on traditional values, 84 percent of the people are opposed to the elitist demand that the drug be legalized.[20]

Before leaving this area of religion and morality, we should observe that the American people have been more sensible on civil rights than either the old-guard conservatives or the elitist leftists. They have unwaveringly rejected institutionalized segregation, yet they have never favored the elitist position of "equality of result." Thus, the polls show that Americans have consistently favored equal rights for Negroes in the areas of voting and education, but have opposed employment quotas and busing by margins approaching eight to one.[21]

From these statistics it becomes apparent that the American citizenry is still very much committed to what may be described as a conservative position on the so-called social issues. Americans believe in God, Judeo-Christian morality, and traditional concepts of crime control. They will listen to legitimate calls for justice. Sadly, due to the leftist domination of the media, these facts are mostly overlooked. The American people are caught up in an extremely frustrating situation. They are conservatives but their nation's right wing refuses to acknowledge their demands and needs.

The Determined People

In the areas of internal security, public orthodoxy, and foreign policy the American people are likewise solidly conservative,

137

though perhaps a bit unrealistic about the nature of international relations. As much is to be expected, for the average American's commitment to fair play, frankness, and the side of the underdog makes it hard for him to fathom the intricacies of foreign affairs. As we will soon see, this shortcoming is due to a certain naiveté on the part of the citizenry. It is not a symptom of the relativist pacifism peddled by the leftist elite.

Internal security and the general preservation of the public orthodoxy are two areas where the average American has remained essentially impervious to the propaganda of leftist elites in the media and academy. During their heyday, Americans approved of loyalty oaths for government workers by seven- and eight-to-one majorities (see, for example, Gallup, March 1949).* The House Un-American Activities Committee, later the House Committee on Internal Security, was long the target of liberal polemicists, who recently succeeded in abolishing it. Despite this consistent leftist animosity to the committee, the American people have always wished to continue it in existence by margins at times approaching four to one (see, for example, Gallup, January 1949). Ideals such as "freedom of speech," "freedom of the press," and the like have never been unconditionally endorsed by the citizenry, which has always been willing to put limits on the rights of persons bent upon weakening the national faith. By a three-to-one margin Americans oppose even a *resigned* Communist teaching at an institute of higher learning.[22] Sixty percent of even the nation's labor leaders (long viewed as supporters of leftist dogmas) would "deny a Communist the right to teach in a college or university."[23] In fact, 50 percent of them would deny a socialist this right as well![24] And Americans are concerned about the dangers posed by alien ideologies not only in government and the academy, but in the nation at large. They have always balked at allowing Communists or those who "attack other races" to give public speeches and 33 percent would forbid newspapers "to criticize our form of government."[25] One-quarter of the nation would go so far as to "forbid a Socialist party from publishing a newspaper."[26] It thus becomes apparent that Americans regard the freedoms of the republican form of gov-

*It is difficult to examine popular attitudes on an issue over long periods of time because as the liberal advance continues, conservatives no longer defend their earlier positions. So the pollsters no longer question people about them. We can only show that on issues that have divided the country over the years, the people have been conservative.

ernment as by no means absolute. They want to preserve the country's consensus on basic questions, just as conservatives have sought to do throughout the nation's history.

The complexities of foreign policy baffle even the experts. In this area the instinctual conservatism of the typical citizen is a sometimes erratic guide. For example, the American people have a long tradition of opposing any sort of offensive action against other nations. Whether it was the Mexican War or the Spanish-American War, the First or the Second World War, the people always opposed intervention until the enemy had struck the first blow.* Americans also seem to oppose intervention, diplomatic or propagandistic, in the affairs of other nations. Accordingly, the liberation policy of fifties conservatism was never supported by more than 10 percent of the American people. But this was not due to any weakness in the people's determination to fight Communism. When Americans perceive their own involvement as a defensive measure, they will go to war. In November 1961 Americans said by a three-to-one margin that they would favor our "fighting our way into Berlin" if the East Germans should close the city.[27] Another poll revealed that the people would support an invasion of Berlin even though they believed that "the Soviet Union would intervene."[28] This attitude has continued throughout the Cold War.

It would seem that the Left has understood the national psyche in this respect far better than the Right. When President Wilson and his advisors had decided that war with Germany was inevitable, they did not openly say so to the people but kept up their neutrality rhetoric until an incident could be created and portrayed to the citizenry as a German offensive. By the same token, Roosevelt, while promising not to involve the country in foreign wars, maneuvered diplomatically so as to antagonize both Japan and Germany.** Presidents Kennedy and Johnson proceeded in like manner to commit America to the Vietnam War. The Right's frankness

*Whether the enemies in each or, indeed, in any of these wars had actually struck the first blow is beyond our present context. The people *thought* they had.

**I am drawing no conclusion about the wisdom of Wilson's and Roosevelt's policies. Nor am I attempting to weigh the importance of Colonel House's fervor for war or Roosevelt's prior knowledge of Japanese preparations to attack Pearl Harbor. I am simply saying that they knew that high-level diplomacy must remain, in a democracy as it always was in other societies, secretive.

139

on foreign policy has been a source of its unpopularity. Realistically, there was no need for fifties conservatives to try to sell their strategy directly to a public that was blissfully ignorant of how world affairs are managed. Now, I realize that the mere suggestion that an American politician should cater to the mythology of the land in order to get elected and then proceed to act as he sees fit once in office is viewed in contemporary America as rank heresy. Be that as it may, the Founding Fathers of the Republic did not believe that the nation's leaders were bound to follow every popular whim. In fact, the foreign policy of our government has always functioned somewhat independently of public opinion. There is so much secrecy, classified information, and diplomatic wheeling-and-dealing in international politics that the ordinary citizen has an exceptionally poor perspective from which to view the problems.

In other areas of national life—the defense of traditional faith and morality, the preservation of internal security and American principles, the movement for a humane capitalism—the people can easily see cause and effect. It is easy to see, for example, that a committed Communist or atheist ensconced in the schools or the government can pose a danger to the nation's well-being. But it is not easy to see the importance of maintaining an anti-Communist government in Chile or preserving the current South African regime. It would seem that in foreign policy conservatives can go only so far in appealing to the American people by plainly stating their principles. Of course, conservatives must boldly advance those parts of their program which already commend themselves to the American mentality. They must be prepared at all times to expose the evil nature of Communism and the barbarism of its leaders. They must emphasize that the Cold War is a constant struggle in which confrontations often occur and that America must be prepared to defend its interests at such times. The CIA, the FBI, congressional investigatory committees, and the nation's military have all enjoyed the support of the American people until recently, and conservatives must propagandize with originality to see that these institutions are restored to their proper position of respect and dignity in society.

In those areas of foreign policy where conservative goals can generate only lukewarm support from the populace, the Right should exercise prudence in marketing its positions. What rightists must remember is that once foreign conflicts arise, whether "hot" or "cold" confrontations, the American people stand behind their government. Even in Vietnam, where public support for American involvement was eroded over the years by the steady propaganda of the leftist media, the American people would have preferred at almost any point to carry the war to the North and win it, as opposed to withdrawal, "Vietnamization," or anything else.[29] Practically speaking, therefore, the Right must publicly advocate "peace through strength," "preparedness," or something similar while conservatives in actual policy-making positions pursue traditional rightist foreign-policy goals.

What should these goals be? Ideally—that is, from a purely speculative point of view—the conservative must favor a foreign policy that ultimately aims at destroying or significantly modifying governments that oppress traditional religion and deprive human beings of their basic dignities. From a practical point of view, of course, prudence should dictate the most advantageous means of pursuing such goals. A realistic conservative foreign policy today would not necessarily be the Teddy Roosevelt type that fifties conservatives advocated. It could bring to bear all the tricks and all the wisdom that traditionalist diplomats have employed throughout history. Negotiations, treaties, revolutions, subversion, propaganda, temporary conciliations, and other methods could and should all be employed. A classical conservative foreign policy pursues its idealistic goals in a realistic manner.

Summary

It should be evident by now that the Right has not been defeated in America because of the inherent liberalism of the populace. Two tenets of postwar conservatism served to discredit it in the eyes of Americans: first, its opposition to public charity and second, its shrill articulation of foreign-policy goals. Today, however, the situation has changed considerably. The Right, having more or less abandoned these two positions, has merely to change its public imagery in order to appeal to the essential conservatism of the people. Conservatism as we defined it in Chapters 2 and 3 is not duty bound to defend its own earlier symbolizations, but merely to counter the ever recurring heresies of relativism and ideology and to ensure that societies function in a stable traditionalist manner.

Rightists can pursue these goals in America by changing their public imagery to suit the times while remaining firm in their allegiance to the first principles of conservatism.

America is wide open for a Disraeli-style revival of conservatism. The people yearn for it and the times demand it. Indeed, should traditionalist conservatives fail to lead this revival and temper it with the insights of orthodox faith and with the inherited wisdom of the West, it could conceivably degenerate into a crude and uncontrollable populism.

Saving Taiwan and the
6 Unborn with
National Health
Insurance

What are the prospects for the future? There is no reason, at this point in the discussion, to give a glibly optimistic answer. The American Right has intoxicated itself for years on the heady brew of self-deception. Let us be frank and clearly assess the realities of our epoch in history. The following facts should be known to conservatives: (1) The Communist world empire is relentlessly expanding. Communist leaders show little or no sign of relaxing their efforts to extend their sphere of control throughout the world. (2) The Third World is emerging as an extremely potent force in international affairs. For the most part, Third World ideologies are antagonistic to the West. (3) The old powers of the Western world—Portugal, Spain, Austria, England, and so on—have lost their global influence while the United States, their obvious heir, has not mustered the internal fortitude necessary to defend the civilization it represents. (4) The various denominations of Judaism and Christianity are beset by heretical fifth columns that gnaw at their vitals and render them increasingly incapable of performing their religious and social functions. (5) In America, as in most Western nations, the social hierarchies that normally furnish the country with a value framework and enforce it through education and legitimate exercise of authority—such as the family, the law-enforcement agencies, the schools, and the armed forces—seem paralyzed by self-doubt.

These obvious and alarming facts can be compared with three somewhat heartening signs: (1) A growing segment of the American intellectual community is recognizing that the old liberal-materialist approach to communal and individual problems cannot deliver the results it promised. (2) Despite the almost total leftist control of government, academy, and media in contemporary America, the average citizen remains basically conservative, in a hazy, instinctual manner. (3) Many Americans are ill at ease with a life that lacks any sense of communal and individual purpose. Millions have sought refuge in psychological, oriental mystical, and fundamentalist religious systems.

The difference between the distressing signs and the encouraging ones, of course, is that the former are concrete and already in progress, while the latter are in the purely potential stage. The American citizenry at large, as well as some segments of the academic world, sense that something is wrong, but they are as yet unaware of the direction in which rectification can be found. Therefore, the broad overview of the present era is far from encouraging for conservatives.

Of all the problems confronting the American Right, the most pressing by far is this: Can the deep-seated assumptions and yearnings of the American people be translated into practical policy in time for America to reassert itself in the global confrontations of the future? The answer to this question is by no means clear. Let us look more closely at the at the Right's prospects in three key departments of national life, the political, educational, and religious.

Politics

The political realm, as I have tried to show in the preceding two chapters, holds great potential for a conservative revival *if* American rightists will lay aside some of their decades-old preconceptions. When engaging in politics, conservatives must remember that their prime responsibility is to see that society survives and functions in a stable, traditional manner. To fulfill its mission in modern America, the Right must break out of its public image as the protector of high finance. It must demonstrate a genuine sensitivity to basic human needs.

Who will lead the way? Rightist organizations or periodicals could. So could individual politicians. In fact, however, nobody is pursuing these realistic goals. There is no need to fool ourselves: the conservatism currently being offered by, say, the American Conservative Union or Young Americans for Freedom has an extremely limited appeal, for two reasons. First, it is at present hopelessly vague about its root assumptions and its motivating philosophy. So its practical program is in a state of flux. It no longer wants to roll back the New Deal, balance the budget, or conquer Moscow. Instead, it only wants to … what? Nobody seems to know for sure. Is its prime motivation libertarian? Its stands on school prayer and abortion would seem to contradict such an assumption. Is its prime motivation religious? Even a superficial reading of its publications would show that religion plays a rather insignificant role in its program. Is it interested in community and stability—in combatting the fear and anomie of contemporary Americans? The leading conservative organizations completely ignore these topics. In short, the organizations of the mainstream Right lack both programs and philosophical purpose.

The second reason for the limited appeal of mainstream conservative organizations is that despite their vagueness—which is quite apparent to their fellow rightists—they do create an impression of sorts in the public mind. Bluntly, they are viewed as the defenders of institutionalized wealth. Despite all the New Majority talk in rightist circles, the city dweller still casts his vote for a Daniel Patrick Moynihan over a James Buckley, and for a Jimmy Carter over a Gerald Ford. Except when the Left puts up a raving radical like George McGovern or Charles Goodell, the little guy will regularly choose an old-school liberal over a watered-down symbol of McKinley-Hoover Republicanism.

Ironically, the only large national rightist organization in America that presents a different image to the public is the John Birch Society. *American Opinion* wars with leftists of all types, whether they call themselves capitalists or Communists. It seems to understand the resentment the ordinary American has for the establishment elites that dominate his country. Unfortunately, the John Birch Society suffers from a credibility gap that is unlikely to be overcome. Robert Welch's *The Politician*, the Revilo Oliver articles on the Kennedy assassination (which seem a bit more plausible in light of recent revelations), and the current *Insiders* theory, expounded par excellence in Gary Allen's *None Dare Call It Conspir-*

acy, have shut the John Birch Society out of the arena of public debate. With the elimination of the Society from respectable political discourse, the American Right has lost two elements vital to its success. To begin with, the efforts of huge numbers of dedicated, self-sacrificing conservatives have been channeled out of areas where these people could have seriously influenced their countrymen. The typical Bircher is not the "dough conservative" of popular conception. He could have taken some of the tarnish off the public image of the American Right.

The second point—which one fears has been overlooked by mainstream rightists—is that the removal of the John Birch Society from the mainstream has weakened feelings of patriotism on the Right. Without a resurgence of heartfelt patriotism, I see little hope for a conservative political revival in America. So-called old-fashioned patriotism, which reveres the legends and stories, heroes, sagas, and songs, the flag and indeed the land itself, has been sadly lacking in "respectable" conservative ranks. Yet both the intelligentsia and the rank-and-file of the John Birch Society possess a vibrant patriotism, which could easily capture the fancy of the citizenry and unify the nation. Medford Evans, Taylor Caldwell, the late E. Merrill Root, and Welch himself get high marks for their exuberant love of country, but unfortunately their work will never stir the masses because the mainstream Right has excluded the John Birch Society from polite company.

Mainstream conservatism, it seems, is unwilling to recast itself in order to appeal to the average citizen. "True believer" periodicals such as *Human Events* stubbornly deny the validity of the New Majority theory, preferring to war against the clear consensus of forty years of American history. *National Review* has charted a somewhat different course. It has jettisoned fifties conservatism, but despite some rumblings of late from Jeffrey Hart and William Rusher it is still essentially a faceless magazine in search of a new conservative form with which to express itself.

The political scene is equally disheartening. There is *no* conservative politician of national stature who seems even faintly aware of the direction in which the Right must go.* Neither the old guard of

*Although his candidacy touched on some of the points we have discussed, Governor Wallace was an unsuitable vehicle for a conservative revival. His openly racist imagery and vituperative rhetoric were far too crude to appeal to anything but a small minority of the populace. Limiting his program to issues like "law and order" and busing, Wallace set goals

rightist politicians, personified by Senators Goldwater and Tower, nor the supposedly newer heroes such as Senator Jesse Helms or Representatives Steve Symms and Phil Crane have recognized the limited appeal of the conservative position as currently articulated.

Does this mean that the American Right must radically change direction and abandon both its leaders and their policies entirely? Not at all. To do so would be practically absurd and philosophically unsound. For better or worse, the fifteen to twenty senators and fifty to eighty representatives who adhere to McKinley-Hoover Republicanism also advocate a strong foreign policy and seek to defend traditional religion and morality. Thus, for the time being, until the New Majority can produce its own leaders, the Right must realistically accept the old-guard conservatives as the leaders of the movement, entitled to our wholehearted support.

Anyway, there is no reason why a more humanistic symbolization of rightism could not incorporate much of the contemporary conservative position on economic matters. Antistatism of the doctrinaire libertarian variety is foolish and perhaps immoral. But once the Right has persuaded Americans that it, too, is capable of dealing compassionately with the basic economic needs of the unfortunate, it can go back to such popular fifties themes as bureaucratic corruption, welfare fraud, rising taxes, and government invasion of personal privacy. The American people are quite friendly to the idea of "starving a fat bureaucrat," despite their endorsement of social security and medicare. If the Right were no longer suspect on the issue of elemental welfarism, conservatives could translate the documented public resentment of government into electoral victories.

Can the Right break its long losing streak? Yes—if one of the big-name conservative organizations, periodicals, or politicians switches to a more realistic conservative stance. It seems unlikely, however, that the groups and individuals now leading the American Right will seize the initiative; they are very much tied up in the vested interests of the post–World War II conservative revival. In all probability, reform will have to come from some new source. A politician could step forward embodying both the doctrinal and personal requirements for success in the electoral climate of the seventies. What sort of man would this new conservative leader be?

---

for himself that were too narrow to generate support among a majority of the voters.

In the first place, his style would have to identify him unmistakably with the "common man." He would need both humor and humility and a willingness to communicate with West Virginian miners, Canarsie tenement dwellers, and Pittsburgh steelworkers. He would have to enjoy (or at least give the appearance of enjoying) crowds, hand shaking, parades, press conferences, and all the rituals of mass-suffrage democracy in a way that neither Landon, Taft, nor Goldwater ever did. He would have to show a fervent loyalty to traditional faith and old-school patriotism—not like a granite-faced Puritan but with sincere emotion and compassion. He would stand four-square against the *abuses* of the welfare state and four-square in favor of its *legitimate* practices. He would court the approval of special-interest groups like labor or ethnic minorities, but not in the manner of the liberal establishment, which caves in to their every demand; he would separate the justifiable from the absurd. Ideally, he would have risen from humble origins and thus could quite literally fulfill his image projection. These criteria are also applicable *mutatis mutandis* to new rightist organizations or journals.

In sum, the political realm is by far the easiest of the three major areas of national life for conservatives to penetrate. As long as the American people remain basically conservative, rightists can continue to reach around media and academy to convey their ideas to the people, as Franklin D. Roosevelt did so adeptly during his career in the public forum. But they must realize from the outset that their defense of the old economic order is their major political liability.

The Academy

The educational system of America is probably the most critical battleground between Right and Left in our time. The minds that will ultimately lead the nation are formed in the universities, high schools, and grade schools of America. How can conservatives take back the nation's schools? Unity and realism are again the central requirements. Party-line conservatism has been the Right's undoing here as well.

There is a growing revolt in the academic world against the once widely acclaimed ideologies of the Left. The *Public Interest* and

Commentary are only the tips of this iceberg. Many who were zealous liberals short decades ago now understand that the forces of relativism and ideology that they unleashed in their "daring" challenges to tradition of any sort have gotten out of control. The old liberals of America did not want their materialistic value-free philosophies to destroy authority and order in society, as is happening now in the legal system, the morality, the foreign policy, and the education of the nation. When in earlier days they preached unlimited freedom on all fronts, they only meant to challenge the shallow conservatism of their contemporaries, not to render school, church, and government utterly impotent. Thus, at present there is a certain restlessness in the ivory tower. It would seem an appropriate time for the rightist scholarly community to wrest leadership of the educational control centers from the followers of Jean-Paul Sartre, Herbert Marcuse, and Norman Brown.

Of course, this task is immensely difficult because most academicians mistrust the Right's commitment to justice, compassion, and other favorite leftist concerns. To regain its losses in this field, the Right must stress those features of conservative doctrine which could catch the fancy of the moderate liberal thinker. Humanism is a vague term, but it suits this context; it refers to *a commitment to the needs of man.* Only conservatives can be consistent humanists, because they alone recognize the eternally binding character of morality and ethics, which is the ultimate justification for humanism. The encyclicals of a number of twentieth-century popes would be a good example of this sort of moral humanism, except that they lack the firmness that a conservative humanism must have. Conservative intellectuals must come across as men who, because of their firm metaphysical or empirical commitment, are interested in helping humanity—not remaking humanity—and wish to relieve some of its agonies. Whether the question is teacher-student or parent-child relations, crime, welfare reform, or world poverty, conservatives have in fact a tremendously appealing position, which I would label "compassionate firmness." The rightist can call for charity and still demand that justice be meted out and authority upheld. Because of its firm value framework, conservatism can be humane without being sentimental. This is how the traditionalist Right can commend itself to an intellectual world, tired of leftist cliches, that is looking for some system of values without having to abandon its devotion to the "cause of man."

149

The Church

The poor image projection of conservatives has done untold harm to traditional religion, too. The rightist elements of the major faiths must learn to apply the major themes of the New Majority philosophy to their work. Conservative religious leaders must perform the twin task of steadfastly defending orthodoxy and simultaneously involving themselves in legitimate social concerns. Thus, the Catholic conservative must combine uncompromising defense of *Humanae Vitae*, and unyielding opposition to women's ordination and liturgical reform, with an honest concern for both the spiritual and material life of, for example, ghetto dwellers, prison inmates, and especially the middle class with its fears of everything from hospitalization to street crime. The average Catholic, Protestant, or Jew does not care a fig about "reforming" or "updating" his faith. Here, too, the field is open for serious conservatives to seize the hour and capitalize on public dissatisfaction with liberal religion. Unfortunately, up to the present the layman has only known a liberal clergy without faith and a conservative clergy without compassion.

Of course, this policy of conservative humanism cannot be followed by "rightists" who, as Thomas Molnar has described it, already have "their hearts half on the other side." To support the justifiable demands of a man-centered age while steadfastly opposing those which are errant is a delicate matter. Indeed, it is possible only for conservatives who realize that *every* age is God centered despite popular misconceptions to the contrary. The task of bringing about a conservative religious revival belongs to those who realize that there is an unbridgeable gulf between faith and heresy, morality and immorality, and that the good cannot be confused with the evil. This remnant of genuinely conservative clergy and laymen are duty bound *because* of the firmness of their commitment, not in spite of it, to present an appealing face to the modern era.

Pragmatism or Truth?

Now for a question that touches on the basic thesis of this work: Is the humanistic revival of conservatism that has been called for here merely a pragmatic policy calculated to improve the fortunes of the Right or is it the natural result of conservative first principles

150

applied to the temporal realm? The answer to this question is that there is no such thing as a natural temporal game plan for conservatism that is eternally binding, for historical circumstances change and the translation of conservatism into practice must change with them. In a saner age the conservative is presented with many legitimate areas of emphasis through which to express his fundamental values. He can choose between the old order of McKinley or the new one of Bryan, between corporate nationalism or monarchial decentralization, or, to cite an example from the purely religious realm, between the Franciscan or Dominican approach to evil. All things being equal, the conservative is free to choose among the alternatives. In our era, though, *all things are not equal.* Therefore, the rightist's prime responsibility is not to follow the promptings of his emotions but to struggle realistically for the survival of the fundamental values that underlie his entire philosophy. This can best be accomplished, I believe, along the lines already suggested. Conservative humanism is one of many legitimate conservative symbolizations, but I am convinced it is the most effective one at this juncture in history.

The Future

Through politics, education, and religion societies are governed in the broader sense of the term. The media, of course, are only the result of the educational system. American conservatism, for all the profundity of its thinkers and dedication of its rank-and-file, has not significantly influenced the nation's direction in recent decades. The Right has maintained isolated pockets of resistance to the leftist domination of the country, but it has played the role of Don Quixote. It has not been a serious national force.

Mortal man is required to do what he can in defense of the good, even if his defense is doomed to defeat. It has been my contention in this volume, however, that the American Right is far from doomed. The masses of people in all parts of the nation still believe, though hazily, in the main principles of conservatism. What is more, the leftist elitists have signally failed to defend Western civilization either at home or abroad. The time is ripe for the Right to cast off an outdated imagery and step forward in American life. Can the American Right galvanize itself in time to save the West from collapse? History will tell us what God already knows.

Notes

Chapter 1

1. Here, as elsewhere in the book, I apply the term mainstream conservative to those rightists generally associated with such publications as *National Review, Human Events,* the *Alternative* (now the *American Spectator*), and *Conservative Digest.* Outside the mainstream, for these purposes, are such diverse philosophies as the extreme (to Americans) Catholic conservatism of *Triumph* (although many of its theoreticians, including L. Brent Bozell, its guiding light, would reject the label "conservative" in its Anglo-Saxon context) and the hard-hitting conservatism of the so-called radical right, best represented by *American Opinion.*

2. "What Next?" *National Review,* December 22, 1972, p. 1287.

3. R. Emmett Tyrrell, Jr. to the editor, *National Review,* December 8, 1972, p. 1330.

4. William F. Buckley, Jr., *The Governor Listeth* (New York: Putnam's, 1970), p. 134.

5. *ibid.,* p. 135.

6. *ibid.,* p. 136.

7. Donald Atwell Zoll, "The Future of American Conservatism: A New Revival?" *Modern Age,* Winter 1974, p. 3.

8. Frank S. Meyer, "On What Ball?" *National Review,* January 4, 1958, p. 17.

9. Frederick D. Wilhelmsen, "Towards a Theology of Survival," *National Review,* January 12, 1965, p. 17.

10. Senator John Tower, *A Program for Conservatives* (New York: McFadden, 1962), p. 32.

11. "The Magazine's Credenda," *National Review,* November 19, 1956, p. 6.

12. Buckley, *Governor Listeth,* pp. 135, 137–138.

13. "C. D. Exclusive: An Interview with William F. Buckley, Jr.," *Conservative Digest,* November 1975, p. 7.

14. George Nash, *The Conservative Intellectual Movement in America since 1945* (New York: Basic Books, 1976).

15. *ibid.*, pp. 322–23 and 343–44 and the notes thereto.

16. I say "respectable" because the Robert Welches, Dan Smoots, and Phoebe Courtneys of what will be described later as the "remnant" of fifties conservatism still defend the positions of the earlier years. Sadly, they have also gone beyond their talk of the International Communist Conspiracy, which was essentially true to the facts of our times. Welch, with the assistance of such *American Opinion* writers as Alan Stang and Gary Allen, has led the way to the discovery of a world-wide conspiracy of *Insiders* who control not only Communism, but international finance, the Council on Foreign Relations, the Bilderbergers, the Bavarian Illuminati, etc. (Believers in the "Master Conspiracy" theory claim that Welch did not, in fact, change his thinking from the days of the *Blue Book* and ordinary anti-Communism. He only hesitated, they explain, before exposing the real powers lurking in the shadows of Moscow and Washington, in order not to shock the public.)

There is a certain degree of truth to the new theory. For religious conservatives there can be no doubt that the extreme laissez-faire capitalism of the early liberals, which peaked in America in the Gilded Age, is just as much in conflict with the truths of traditional faith as is socialism or Communism. In fact, this point has been made repeatedly by various popes in their social encyclicals of the past eighty years. So in a sense the forces of secularism are united, if not by conspiracy, then by the common effect of their workings in history. As L. Brent Bozell once wrote of the Birchite thesis, ". . . the typical Bircher knows . . . that the One behind the desk [of the Master Conspiracy] or lurking in a back room . . . is a Spirit, for whom there is only one rebuff. Begone . . ." (*Triumph,* October 1971, p. 31).

17. L. Brent Bozell, "Letter to Yourselves," Part I, *Triumph,* January 1976, p. 20. (Originally appeared in *Triumph* of March 1969.)

18. *ibid.*

19. William F. Buckley, Jr., *Inveighing We Will Go* (New York: Putnam's, 1971), p. 69.

20. "A Clarification," *National Review,* September 7, 1957, p. 149.

21. "Why the South Must Prevail," *National Review,* August 24, 1957, p. 199.

22. Barry Goldwater, *The Conscience of a Conservative* (Shepherdsville, Ky.: Victor Publishing, 1960), p. 34.

23. ibid., p. 36.

24. "The Court Views Its Handiwork," *National Review,* September 21, 1957, p. 244.

25. "The Tank as Educator," *National Review,* September 22, 1956, p. 6.

26. "So It Goes," *National Review,* September 24, 1963, p. 221.

27. Barry Goldwater, *Where I Stand* (New York: McGraw-Hill, 1962), p. 39.

28. "Text of Goldwater Speech on Rights," *New York Times,* June 19, 1964, p. 18.

29. Goldwater, *Conscience,* p. 36.

30. "Goldwater Speech on Rights," *loc. cit.*

31. Buckley, *Inveighing,* p. 42.

32. Goldwater, *Conscience,* p. 118.

33. *ibid.,* p. 122.

34. *ibid.,* p. 94.

35. *ibid.,* p. 99.

36. *ibid.,* p. 106.

37. *ibid.,* p. 120.

38. *ibid.,* p. 121.

39. *ibid.,* p. 120.

40. "The Hungary Pledge," *National Review,* December 8, 1956, p. 5.

41. "Abstractions Kill the West," *National Review,* December 8, 1956, pp. 6, 7.

42. Goldwater, *Conscience,* p. 121.

43. "Verdict on Hungary," *National Review,* July 6, 1957, p. 29.

44. "Keep the Pot Boiling," *National Review,* July 20, 1957, p. 77.

45. Barry Goldwater, "A Foreign Policy for America," *National Review,* March 25, 1961, p. 181.

46. "Evangelistic" is Buckley's word to describe the anti-Communism of the fifties Right. Burnham himself would probably reject the label. His own reasons for advocating victory over Communism were more pragmatic.

47. James Burnham, *The Struggle for the World* (New York: John Day, 1947), p. 230.

48. James Burnham, *Containment or Liberation?: An Inquiry into the Aims of United States Foreign Policy* (New York: John Day, 1953), p. 252.

49. James Burnham, "Liberation: What Next?" *National Review,* January 19, 1957, p. 71.

50. James Burnham, "Why Not Some Yankee Trading?" *National Review,* September 15, 1972, p. 998.

51. Burnham, *Struggle,* p. 247.

52. Ronald Reagan, *The Creative Society* (New York: Devin-Adair, 1968), p. 57.

53. Ronald Reagan with Charles D. Hobbs, *Ronald Reagan's Call to Action* (New York: Warner Books, 1976), pp. 42–43.

54. Erik von Kuehnelt-Leddihn, *Leftism* (New Rochelle, N.Y.: Arlington House, 1975), p. 406.

55. Kevin Phillips, "The Future of American Politics," *National Review,* December 22, 1972, p. 1398.

56. Thurmond, to his credit, remained officially neutral during the 1976 Reagan effort.

57. William A. Rusher, "What's Happened to Barry," *Conservative Digest*, April 1976, p. 16.

58. *Congressional Record*, April 8, 1957, pp. 5258, 5259, 5260.

59. "So Long, Ike," *National Review*, January 14, 1961, pp. 8, 9.

60. Zoll, "Future of American Conservatism," p. 3.

61. Bozell, "Letter," p. 20.

62. The new organization formed by Howard Phillips and Meldrim Thomson, the Conservative Caucus, appears to be far more dynamic and politically imaginative than the run-of-the-mill "true believer" organizations. Despite its energy, though, it is plagued by the same ills that afflict the YAF-ACU contingent. It offers a modified fifties conservatism (although perhaps not quite so watered down as the normative groups) and, while constantly harping on the need to establish links with ethnic Democrats, disenchanted fifties liberals, and others, has done very little, either doctrinally or practically, to facilitate such a connection.

63. Nash, *Conservative Intellectual Movement*, p. 274.

64. *ibid.*, pp. 322, 323.

65. See *ibid.*, pp. 320–334.

66. It would probably be interesting for mainstream rightists to look into their own ranks and see how many of those subscribing to publications such as *Human Events* and *National Review* are simultaneously associated with the so-called "radical right." My own experiences have indicated that outside of a certain intellectual elite, the rank and file conservative is likely to be just as devoted to Robert Welch as to William Buckley, just as partisan for George Wallace as for Ronald Reagan.

67. "The John Birch Society and the Conservcative Movement," *National Review*, October 19, 1965, pp. 914–920, 925–929.

68. Nash, *Conservative Intellectual Movement*, p. xi. Nash claims that the contribution of the "remnant" to conservatism as an intellectual force was "negligible." The statement is true for the most part, but can one safely say that E. Merrill Root and Revilo P. Oliver (despite their occasional wild eccentricities—especially in Oliver's case) added nothing of consequence to conservatism with their writings? Is not Root's collection of essays, *America's Steadfast Dream* (Belmont, Mass.: Western Islands, 1971), a deeply moving presentation of conservative beliefs?

69. Mainstream rightists find the Birch Society guilty of inferring "subjective motives from objective consequences" (the phrase is Buckley's) and believe that Birchers suffer from a veritable "psychosis of conspiracy" (the phrase is Frank Meyer's). I tend to agree with the mainstreamers' rejection of Birchite theories; but to question their conservative credentials on this basis is unnecessarily schismatic and self-limiting. Do mainstream liberals read Norman Mailer out of the intellectual forum for writing preposterous nonsense about the CIA ("A Harlot High and

Low: Reconnoitering through the Secret Government," *New York,* August 16, 1976)? This piece puts to shame anything Revilo Oliver wrote about The Company in *American Opinion* in the aftermath of the Kennedy assassination ("Marxmanship in Dallas," *American Opinion,* February 1964, continued in March 1964). The European Right, though capable of great profundity, has never ceased to utter silly drivel about international bankers, Jews, and Freemasons. Does this make French or Spanish or Italian conservatism illegitimate manifestations of the Right? Was Action Française liberal or conservative? Are the Carlists outside the rightist camp? Conspiracy theories are (usually) foolish, but adherence to them in is no way a denial of basic conservatism.

70. In the case of the JBS this has of course been transformed into "victory over the *Insiders.*"

71. The descendants of Wallaceism, the American Party and the American Independent Party, have returned to the philosophy of "remnant" conservatism as personified by former Congressman John Schmitz.

72. Anderson certainly has a much firmer grasp on the meaning of fifties conservatism than does Maddox, who came to the political Right rather late in his career.

73. "Republicans, 1976," *National Review,* September 3, 1976, p. 939.

74. Jeffrey Hart, "Earthquake Time in America," *National Review,* March 3, 1976, p. 211.

75. William Rusher, *The Making of the New Majority Party* (New York: Sheed and Ward, 1975), p. 37.

76. *ibid.,* p. 118.

77. On the issue of federal income taxation, for example, conservatives first (in the early 1900s) were *completely* opposed to it and hailed the Supreme Court decisions that declared early attempts to enact the levy unconstitutional. Later, during the conservative revival of the fifties, mainstream rightists limited their critique to the graduated features of taxation. (Goldwater in *The Conscience* wanted to abolish all graduated income tax laws.) Finally, today normative conservatives seem just to want lower taxes and somewhat larger deductions or loopholes for capital interests. (As always, the "remnant" or "radical right" has continued to defend the original barricades and calls for a repeal of the Sixteenth Amendment.) Does yesterday's liberalism inevitably become today's conservatism, while yesterday's conservatism becomes today's reactionism?

In the area of internal security conservatives have retreated from defending Palmer and Daugherty, to defending the Smith Act, to defending the very existence of Senate Internal Security Subcommittee and the House Committee on Internal Security. Par for the course, they have lost every battle.

The rightist position on suffrage has gone from a defense of legislative election of senators, to opposition to women's suffrage, to defending the poll tax, to defending literacy tests, to opposing the Supreme Court reapportionment decisions. Again, losing causes all.

156

Conservatives can well sigh together with William F. Buckley, Jr., who said that apparently victory for rightist causes "is beyond our reach. Perhaps it was meant to be so."

78. The late Willmoore Kendall somehow believed that the Right in America had defeated the Left on all "important" issues. Buckley has called this view "puzzling," which in my opinion is an understatement. Kendall's view is, on the face of it, absurd. It is indeed fascinating how Kendall, who penetratred to the core of almost any topic he tangled with, could have entertained such a belief. Perhaps the answer lies in the question itself; it was a *belief*. Kendall loved America and he especially loved its people. He *believed* them to be a virtuous people. (Of course, he had to, for his entire philosophical comprehension of the American system was grounded in his concept of an essentially good citizenry watched over by the remnant of a cultural elite whose task it was to keep them good.) This *faith* in the goodness of Americans simply would not allow him to see that the people themselves, through Congress, were guiding the land leftward. As the Biblical prophet Habakkuk said, "The righteous man liveth by his faith."

79. Russell Kirk, *The Conservative Mind* (New York: Avon Books, 1968; published by arrangement with Henry Regnery, Chicago), p. 14.

80. Thomas Molnar, *The Counter-Revolution* (New York: Funk and Wagnalls, 1969), p. 158.

81. Voegelin may be compared to a master quarterback, who, having marched his team triumphantly down the field, fumbles the ball away with first and goal to go from the one. For all his monumental work, his treatment of the *truthfulness* of Judeo-Christian teachings in Volume IV of his magnum opus *Order and History* (*The Ecumenic Age* [Baton Rouge: Louisiana State University Press, 1975]) must rank as the most significant philosophical fumble that the conservative team has had to endure in a long time.

82. After all, Pilsudski, Horthy, Dollfuss, Mussolini, Franco, and Salazar did rule for a while.

83. Told to me by Hallowell in a telephone conversation.

84. Von Kuehnelt-Leddihn, *Leftism*, p. 419.

85. Erik von Kuehnelt-Leddihn, "Retrospective and Prophecy," *National Review,* December 5, 1975, p. 1349.

86. Molnar, *Counter-Revolution*, p. 202.

Chapter 2

1. Jeffrey Hart, *The American Dissent* (Garden City, N.Y.: Doubleday, 1966), p. 221.

2. Peter Viereck, *Conservatism Revisited* (Glencoe, Ill.: Free Press, 1965), p. 155.

3. "The Magazine's Credenda," *National Review*, November 19, 1955, p. 6.

4. Frank S. Meyer, " 'Slippage' and the Theory of the Lesser Evil," *National Review*, February 28, 1959, p. 556.

5. Jeffrey Hart, "Peter Berger's Paradox," *National Review*, May 12, 1972, p. 512.

6. M. Stanton Evans, "A Conservative Case for Freedom," in Frank S. Meyer, ed., *What Is Conservatism?* (New York: Holt, Rinehart and Winston, 1964), pp. 67–78.

7. *ibid.*, p. 71.

8. *ibid.*, p. 69.

9. M. Stanton Evans, "Varieties of Conservative Experience," *Modern Age*, Spring 1971, p. 137.

10. Frank S. Meyer, "Freedom, Tradition and Conservatism," in Meyer, ed., *What Is Conservatism?*, p. 14.

11. *ibid.*, pp. 18, 19.

12. Frank S. Meyer, *The Conservative Mainstream* (New Rochelle, N.Y.: Arlington House, 1969), p. 426.

13. Meyer, ed., *What Is Conservatism?*, p. 13.

14. Meyer, *Conservative Mainstream*, p. 425.

15. Frank S. Meyer, *In Defense of Freedom* (Chicago: Henry Regnery, 1962), pp. 6, 7.

16. Meyer, *Conservative Mainstream*, pp. 417, 423, 425.

17. In fairness it should be noted that on page 9 of *In Defense of Freedom* (and only there) Meyer makes some allowance for other forms of conservatism outside of the Anglo-Saxon tradition. He writes:

> The representative democratic institutions, combined with constitutional guarantees of freedom, which have been the matrix for the development of free societies in the United States, Europe and some other Western nations, may not be the best political forms for the achievement of an approximation of a good society even in all countries of Western civilization, much less elsewhere.

Fortunately for his general thesis, Meyer did not spell out which Western nations require other forms of government. Was he referring to, say, Spain and Portugal? Certainly their fondness (at that time) for "forced virtue" would seem to disqualify these nations as"approximations of a good society." Was he hinting at some form of monarchial restoration in other Western lands? It would seem not, for the "welfarism" of Habsburgs, Hohenzollerns, and others is a kind of "economic collectivism," which Meyer tells us (page 109) is "dedicated to the principled suppression of the freedom of man . . ." So it would appear that Meyer's one-paragraph flirtation with rightist tolerance simply cannot be reconciled with the overriding theme of his philosophy, which is the portrayal of American constitutional government as the ultimate and only true form of government.

18. De Maistre was a tremendously sloppy political philosopher and is perhaps better described as a cross between a polemicist and a theoretician. He advanced all sorts of contradictory apologetics to justify the *ancien régime*. His occasional utopian musings should be viewed in the total context of his work, which was basically conservative.

19. Eric Voegelin, *From Enlightenment to Revolution* (Durham, N.C.: Duke University Press, 1975), p. 184.

20. See James Burnham, "Notes on Authority, Morality, and Power," *National Review*, December 1, 1970, pp. 1283–1289.

21. See Donald Atwell Zoll, "Shall We Let America Die?" *National Review*, December 16, 1969, pp. 1261–1263.

22. Frank S. Meyer, "What Kind of Order?" *National Review*, December 30, 1969, p. 1327.

23. Frank S. Meyer, "In Re Professor Zoll: Order and Freedom,"*National Review*, March 24, 1970, p. 311.

24. Thomas Molnar, letter to the editor, *National Review*, May 19, 1970, p. 529.

25. Meyer, "In Re Zoll," *ibid.*

26. In recent years Wilhelmsen has almost completely dropped the self-designation "conservative" or "Catholic conservative" from his writings. He now feels that "Orthodox Catholics . . . don't fit anywhere in the philosophical and political dialectic that governs the dying secular order . . ." Accordingly, he cautions that "Christians [must] transcend the dialectic" and not be "sunk" as were the "Carlists [and] . . . the Catholic rising in the Vendée" by being "defined in terms of the dialectical thesis" of revolution and counterrevolution. (Frederick Wilhelmsen, "Transcending the Dialectic," *Triumph*, January 1976, pp. 27, 28. Originally appeared in *Triumph*, September 1969.) Despite these recent disclaimers, Wilhelmsen's thought is in fact a coherent attempt to present truths that in common parlance are referred to as rightist. Wilhelmsen himself today much prefers the label of "traditionalist" to that of conservative.

27. Frederick Wilhelmsen, "The Traditionalist Right," *National Review*, February 22, 1966, p. 172.

28. Frederick Wilhelmsen, "Hallowed Be Thy World," *Triumph*, January 1976, p. 13. Originally appeared in *Triumph*, June 1968.

29. Wilhelmsen, "Transcending the Dialectic," p. 26.

30. Frederick Wilhelmsen, "Toward an Incarnational Politics: Against Despair," *Triumph*, February 1973, pp. 12, 14.

31. Frederick Wilhelmsen, *Hilaire Belloc: No Alienated Man* (New York: Sheed and Ward, 1954), pp. 98–99.

32. Frederick Wilhelmsen, "The Perpetual Itch," *National Review*, August 22, 1967, p. 917.

33. Frederick Wilhelmsen, "The Conservative Vision," *Commonweal*, June 24, 1955, p. 297.

34. Frederick Wilhelmsen and Willmoore Kendall, "Cicero and the Politics of the Public Orthodoxy," *Intercollegiate Review,* Winter 1968–69, p. 100.

35. Frederick Wilhelmsen, "The New Voegelin," *Triumph,* January 1975, p. 35.

36. Wilhelmsen, "Conservative Vision," p. 299.

37. Wilhelmsen, "Hallowed Be Thy World," p. 15.

38. Wilhelmsen, *Hilaire Belloc,* p. 93.

39. Wilhelmsen, "Hallowed Be Thy World," p. 16

40. Frederick Wilhelmsen, "Toward an Incarnational Politics: The Hour Is Short, the Hour Is Now," *Triumph,* April 1973, p. 31.

41. *ibid.*

42. *ibid.*

43. Wilhelmsen, "Hallowed Be Thy World," *ibid.*

44. Wilhelmsen, *Hilaire Belloc, ibid.*

45. Frederick Wilhelmsen, "Pope as Icon," *Triumph,* January 1971, p. 11.

46. Wilhelmsen, "Hour Is Short, Hour Is Now," p. 28.

47. Frederick Wilhelmsen, "Donoso Cortes and the Meaning of Political Power," *Intercollegiate Review,* January-February 1967, p. 127.

48. Zoll, "Shall We Let America Die?" p. 1263.

49. Donald Atwell Zoll, *The Twentieth Century Mind* (Baton Rouge: Louisiana State University Press, 1967), pp. 25–47.

50. Donald Atwell Zoll, "Conservatism and a Philosophy of Personality," *Modern Age,* Spring 1960, p. 161.

51. Jeffrey Hart, "David Hume and Skeptical Conservatism," *National Review,* February 13, 1968, p. 132.

52. Zoll, "Conservatism and Philosophy of Personality," p. 163.

53. Zoll, *Twentieth Century Mind,* p. 131.

54. Zoll, "Conservatism and Philosophy of Personality," p. 164.

55. *ibid.,* pp. 163, 166.

56. *ibid.*

57. Donald Atwell Zoll, "The Future of American Conservatism: A New Revival?" *Modern Age,* Winter 1974, pp. 6, 7.

58. *ibid.*

59. *ibid.,* p. 11.

60. Donald Atwell Zoll, "The Ethical Base of Community," *Modern Age,* Summer 1972, p. 255.

61. *ibid.*

62. Zoll, "Future of American Conservatism," pp. 8–9.

63. Donald Atwell Zoll, "Philosophical Foundations of the American Political Right," *Modern Age,* Spring 1971, p. 170.

64. Zoll, "Ethical Base of Community," p. 257.

65. The nonfootnoted references to Zoll's opinions in the preceding

seven paragraphs are derived from a telephone conversation between Professor Zoll and myself, December 23, 1976.

66. Donald Atwell Zoll, "The Prospects for a Conservative Majority," *Modern Age,* Fall 1973, p. 374.

67. Russell Kirk, *The Conservative Mind* (New York: Avon Books, 1968; published by arrangement with Henry Regnery, Chicago), pp. 17, 18, 19.

68. *ibid.*

69. *ibid.*

70. *ibid.,* pp. 45, 46.

71. Willmoore Kendall, *Contra Mundum* (New Rochelle, N.Y.: Arlington House, 1971), pp. 45–46.

72. Thomas Molnar, *The Counter-Revolution* (New York: Funk and Wagnalls, 1969), p. 107.

73. Donald Atwell Zoll, "Of Action and Reaction," *Modern Age,* Summer-Fall 1970, p. 327.

74. Thomas Molnar, "Conservatism and Intelligence," *Intercollegiate Review,* Spring 1974, pp. 74, 75.

75. *ibid.*

76. Molnar, *Counter-Revolution,* p. 90.

77. Molnar, "Conservatism and Intelligence," p. 76.

78. The quotations in the preceding paragraphs are excerpted from various letters I received from Professor Molnar in December 1976 and January 1977. Henceforth all nonfootnoted quotations from Molnar are taken from those letters or from conversations between Professor Molnar and myself.

79. Molnar, *Counter-Revolution,* p. 103.

80. *ibid.,* p. 39.

81. *ibid.,* p. 203.

82. *ibid.,* p. 108.

Chapter 4

1. For information on the 1936 election I have relied heavily on Volume III of *A History of American Presidential Elections, 1789–1968,* ed. by Arthur M. Schlesinger, Jr. (New York: Chelsea House, 1971). The entry on the election of 1936, which includes the texts of important speeches, is by William E. Leuchtenberg.

2. Schlesinger, ed., *History of American Presidential Elections,* Vol. III, p. 2817.

3. *ibid.,* p. 2820.

4. *ibid.*

5. *ibid.,* p. 2817.

6. *ibid.,* p. 2818.

7. *ibid.,* pp. 2898, 2899.

8. *ibid.,* p. 2839.

9. David Hackett Fischer, *The Revolution of American Conservatism* (New York: Harper and Row, 1965), p. 150.

10. James T. Patterson, *Mr. Republican: A Biography of Robert A. Taft* (Boston: Houghton Mifflin, 1971), p. 152.

11. *ibid.,* p. 157.

12. *ibid.,* p. 156.

13. George H. Mayer, *The Republican Party, 1854–1966* (New York, Oxford University Press, 1967), p. 468.

14. Patterson, *Mr. Republican,* p. 159.

15. The 1952 campaign is covered in detail in Patterson, *op. cit.;* Arthur M. Schlesinger, Jr., ed., *The Coming to Power* (New York: Chelsea House, 1972), see "The Election of 1952" by Barton J. Bernstein; and George H. Mayer, *The Republican Party, 1854–1966* (New York: Oxford University Press, 1967).

16. Patterson, *Mr. Republican,* p. 499.

17. George Gallup, *The Gallup Polls, 1935–1971* (New York: Random House, 1972), Vol. II, pp. 1055, 1070, 1057 (Eisenhower vs. Truman, Stevenson, Kefauver); 1022, 1070, 1045 (Taft vs. Truman, Stevenson, Kefauver).

18. *New York Times,* July 1, 1952, p. 22; July 2, 1952, p. 24; July 3, 1952, p. 24.

19. Patterson, *Mr. Republican,* p. 571.

20. Mayer, *Republican Party, 1854–1966,* p. 537.

21. *Newsweek,* October 19, 1964, p. 28.

22. *ibid.*

23. Gallup, *Gallup Polls,* Vol. III, p. 1884.

24. *Newsweek,* October 19, 1964, p. 28.

25. *ibid.,* p. 27.

26. *ibid.*

27. *ibid.*

28. *ibid.,* p. 28.

29. See Robert D. Novak, *The Agony of the GOP, 1964* (New York: Macmillan, 1965), p. 332.

30. Gallup, *Gallup Polls,* Vol. III, p. 1890.

31. *New York Times,* March 25, 1976, p. 30.

Chapter 5

1. George Gallup, *The Gallup Polls, 1935–1971* (New York: Random House, 1972), Vol. I, pp. 40, 52 (NRA); 9 (AAA).

162

2. *Fortune,* July 1935, p. 67.

3. Lloyd Free and Hardy Cantril, *The Political Beliefs of Americans* (New Brunswick, N.J.: Rutgers University Press, 1967), p. 12.

4. Joe R. Feagan, *Subordinating the Poor* (Englewood Cliffs, N.J.: Prentice-Hall, 1975), pp. 134–35.

5. See note 3, *supra.*

6. Hamilton's letter to James A. Bayard, April 1802, quoted in David Hackett Fischer, *The Revolution of American Conservatism* (New York: Harper and Row, 1965), p. 110.

7. Frank Armbruster and Doris Yokelson, *The Forgotten Americans* (New Rochelle, N.Y.: Arlington House, 1972), p. 41.

8. *ibid.,* p. 46.

9. *ibid.,* p. 47.

10. *ibid.,* p. 37.

11. *ibid.,* p. 36.

12. *ibid.,* p. 34.

13. *ibid.,* p. 30.

14. *ibid.,* p. 67.

15. *ibid.,* p. 32.

16. *ibid.,* p. 54.

17. *ibid.,* p. 58.

18. *ibid.,* p. 60.

19. *ibid.,* p. 61.

20. *ibid.,* p. 63.

21. *ibid.,* p. 84.

22. Stuart Chase, *American Credos* (New York: Harper, 1962), p. 156.

23. *ibid.*

24. *ibid.*

25. *ibid.,* p. 154.

26. *ibid.*

27. *ibid.,* p. 53.

28. *ibid.,* p. 54.

29. Robert Chandler, *Public Opinion* (New York: Bowker, 1972).

Index

mined people, 137–141; a
moral people, 135–137
Americans for Constitutional
Action, 32, 46
America's Steadfast Dream,
155
Ames, Fisher, 36, 118–119
Ancien régime, 40, 102, 103,
118, 158
Anderson, Tom, 33, 156
Anti-Communism, 15
Antifederalists, 131
Antistatism, 15
Aristocracy, 104–105
Ashbrook, John, 27
Austria, 143
Authoritarianism, 48

Babbitt, Irving, 129
Batista, Fulgencio, 46
Battle Line, 47
Bavarian Illuminati, 153
Beliefs, ideological, vs. opera-
tional, 133–134
Bilderbergers, 153
Black Belt, 66
Blaine, James, 36
Blue Book, 153
Borah, William, 115
Bozell, L. Brent, 14–15, 30,44,
74, 15, 153
Branden, Nathaniel, 43, 67
Brazil, 46
Bricker, John W., 15, 123
Brown, Norman, 149
*Brown v. Board of Education
of Topeka, Kansas,* 16, 19–
20, 82, 126
Brownson, Orestes, 76
Bryan, William Jennings, 33,

107, 109, 119, 151
Buckley, James, 145
Buckley, William F., Jr., 11–
12, 13–14, 15, 19–20, 23–24,
26, 45, 154, 155, 157
Bull Moosers, 83, 107, 114,
131
Burke, Edmund, 37, 53, 76,
77, 78, 79, 84
Burnham, James, 24–25, 56,
154

Caldwell, Taylor, 146
Calhoun, John, 36
Camelots du Roi, 50
Cantril, Hardy, 133–134
Carlists, 47, 64, 66, 156
Carter, Jimmy, 145
Catholicism, 56, 58–59, 60,
61–62, 95, 136
Change: in America, 108–110,
111–113; through innova-
tion, 106–108; Kirk on, 77,
78; social, 98–102; tradi-
tions and, 102–108; work-
able conservative theory of,
93
Chardin, Teilhard de, 55
Chesterton, G.K., 50
Chiang Kai-shek, 46
Chicago Seven, 137
Child labor, 117, 133
Chile, 46, 140
China, 12, 14, 15, 21, 27, 29
Chodorov, Frank, 44
Christian Crusade, 32
CIA, 140, 156
Civil rights, conservatives
and, 15–21, 123–124
Civil Rights Act of 1964, 18,
19

171